FUGITIVES
of the
HEART

FUGITIVES
of the
HEART

Sins That So Easily Beset Us

Thelma P. Oyesiku

XULON PRESS

Xulon Press
2301 Lucien Way #415
Maitland, FL 32751
407.339.4217
www.xulonpress.com

Paperback ISBN-13: 978-1-66282-407-4
Ebook ISBN-13: 978-1-66282-408-1

DEDICATIONS

To my mother, Jacqueline Ngwenya, whose great sacrifices have opened amazing opportunities in my life. I would not be where I am without a mother like you.

To my family and friends in and out of Zimbabwe, you are a part of me.

To my husband, Christopher you are amazing and supportive in every way, I love you.

To my children who are treasures from God, you fill my heart with joy.

To my spiritual parents Apostles Kevin and Denise Nelson, whose agape love and constant prayer have made me the woman I am today.

To Doria Hickman, you are my sister from another mother. Your family is my family.

To all the members at Abundant Life Church of Erie and the community you are my home away from home.

To the Rock Church and the community, you are our new beginning, we are excited to be part of your story.

To all my brothers and sisters in the faith, near and far, God is fighting for you, keep running the race.

Finally, to the One who made it all possible. The One true God, maker of heaven and earth, who has given us life. Thank you, Jesus, for the ultimate sacrifice to reunite us with Yahweh. We are nothing without you, I am nothing without you. I love you!

TABLE OF CONTENTS

INTRODUCTION

I have always loved the movie with Harrison Ford and Tommy Lee Jones, "The Fugitive." Full of action and suspense, all in the name of a man trying to catch his wife's killer and clear his name. If you have not seen it, check it out, it is one for the books. One day during my meditation time, I heard the words, Fugitives of the Heart. Immediately I was intrigued because 1) all I knew about fugitives was the movie and 2) what was the Father trying to tell me. As I began to ponder these things in my heart, the Lord revealed how we all have things we struggle with within our hearts. These 'struggles' are a combination of past and present decisions, good and bad. While other struggles are contributions that come from your lineage long ago, they flow in your bloodline. The Lord called these struggles fugitives because the blood of the Lamb has outlawed them. They are considered enemies of the throne because they sought to overtake heaven. The Lord was about to reveal that regardless of the struggle (fugitive) source, it was up to us to either yield continuously to them or send them packing.

What is a fugitive?

A fugitive is someone who hides or flees from prosecution, arrest, punishment, justice, enemies, or brutal treatment.

In the Garden of Eden, Adam and Eve hid once they ate the forbidden fruit. In the wake of their sin, hiding was the best way to avoid the Father. We do the same thing; we hide our sins so that the Father doesn't see them. What is even more troubling is that we could be aware of some of our shortcomings but don't bother to do anything about them. The Lord wants to remind us that a little leaven leavens the whole lump (Gal 5:9). If we do not take time to surrender the contents of our hearts to the Father, we will suffer more losses than victories. We will find ourselves repeatedly fighting the same battles in different seasons of our lives. A defeated life does not reflect the goodness of God. In Isaiah 1:19, God says, "If you are willing and obedient, you shall eat the good of the land." God wants you and I to live in victory and eat the good of the land. He wants our lives to radiate His omnipresence in every way. Living in cycles of continual defeat, sin, and iniquitous patterns doesn't reflect God's presence in our lives.

It reflects deep-rooted issues that we have not addressed. I think it is high time we addressed them. The enemy uses sin and curses to keep us bound; this is how cycles happen. But when the Father, Son, and Holy Spirit are truly dwelling in you, no curse can stand a chance! Not even a fraction of one!

What kind of fugitives are there?

There are two kinds of fugitives that inhabit our hearts: default and chosen fugitives.

Default: These fugitives are the inherent package of the flesh; they come with our earthly nature. The Bible lists them in Galatians 5:19-21,

> "Now the works of the flesh are evident, which are: adultery, fornication, uncleanness, lewdness, idolatry, sorcery, hatred, contentions, jealousies, outbursts of wrath, selfish ambitions, dissensions, heresies, envy, murders, drunkenness, revelries, and the like; of which I tell you beforehand, just as I also told you in time past, that those who practice such things will not inherit the kingdom of God."

In Genesis 6:5, the Bible tells us that as humans, our thoughts are evil.

> "...and that every intent of the thoughts of his
> heart was only evil continually."

Chosen: We choose to do and think things that are against the will of God. Romans 1:25 says, "who exchanged the truth of God for the lie...."

Can I have one or the other?

You can have both kinds of fugitives dwelling in your heart. It is either a case of unsaved or saved, but you enjoy being you more than transforming into Christ's nature. You will see in the pages to come how this works.

To better understand the fugitives that the Lord wants us to surrender, we must be open and willing to take this journey with the Holy Spirit. We also need to have the courage to be vulnerable with the Father. He already knows all about you and your struggles. As you read this book, I encourage you to shine God's righteous light in areas where the fugitives may be hiding. Once they are exposed, you may begin or continue the journey of allowing the Holy Spirit to develop your

Christ-like nature. It is incredible how many of us fall into the same traps because we have not put away our old man (2 Cor 5:17). It would appear that some of us are trying to satisfy our flesh and God at the same time. Our God is a jealous God who wants it all; either you are with Him, or you're not. It is time to draw a line in the sand, as the adage says, and surrender fully to the power of the Holy Spirit.

In the movie "The Fugitive," the main character, played by Harrison Ford, was accused of killing his wife. After escaping a prison bus accident, he worked hard to clear his name. I can parallel the movie with the devil and say that the fugitive here is Satan, and he is guilty of all the charges brought against him. Just as hard Harrison Ford's character (Richard Kimble) worked to clear his name, the enemy works just as hard, if not harder, to ruin God's creation. "The thief does not come except to steal, and to kill, and to destroy" *(John 10:10)*. The enemy hates you, but he hates God the most, so he steals, kills, and destroys God's people knowing that it will break the Lord's heart. He has made it his mission to take us out by any means necessary. Hell is not designed for humanity; it is intended for the enemy and the fallen angels. However, due to our disobedience, we were added to the list. Matthew 25:41 states, "Then He will also say to those on the left hand, "Depart from me, you cursed, into the everlasting fire prepared for the devil and his angels."

After beguiling Eve and Adam, Satan used this position as an entry way to hide in our hearts because creation was now compromised. Out of compromise, choices were born in our hearts. We could choose right or wrong; it was and still is our prerogative. Regardless of our choices, God is still on the throne, and Satan is still a fugitive. If you choose to let him stay in your heart, he will bring his fugitive friends along for the journey. Think of his friends as the fruit of a poisonous tree-nothing good can ever come of this kind of fruit.

The kingdom of darkness cannot create anything; it copies what the kingdom of heaven does. Therefore, if you walk with Jesus, you will bear the fruits of righteousness, and if you walk in darkness, you will bear the fruits of darkness. That is why our choices in life matter so much. Choosing darkness has the trifecta effect of sin, iniquity, and transgression. We will discuss the trifecta effect in detail later. However, if you choose Jesus, then by the power of his blood, the fugitive and his friends must vacate your heart. His blood is most effective in annihilating ties with these fugitives so that you can fulfill heaven's mandate for your life. After all, that is why he came, so you could have life in its fullness. (Jn 10:10)

We need to consider that willfully entertaining the enemy and his wiles means that we are participating in our destruction. We cannot afford to ignore the enemy's vices either because the cost is the grave. Jesus already paid the price for our redemption, so we cannot waste his blood by refusing to yield to the reformative change the Holy Ghost brings.

Throughout the book, there will be thought-provoking questions. Strive to answer them honestly. Then there are prayers listed for the issues discussed in specific sections. Lastly, you will see notes about being Christ-like. These notes show us a blueprint on how Jesus dealt with these fugitives. When we honestly and sincerely follow Jesus Christ, we can become more Christ-like- this is our commission from Him.

CHAPTER 1

2020

2020 brought an unexpected, unprecedented sequence of events that rocked the nations to the core. The pandemic took lives, changed establishments, and transformed our way of life. COVID-19 was an epic global reset, and I believe that the Lord used this time to course-correct our lives. I know in my personal life I was running on fumes. Before the pandemic hit, I was elbow deep in motherhood, church activities, per diem work, etc. Just like so many of you, my hectic schedule left me drained. After the pandemic hit, I took the time between homeschooling and surviving the day to re-evaluate my relationship with the Father. I was saved for eighteen years, and I felt like I had nothing to show for it. The contents of my heart did not reflect that eighteen-year union. What happened? I asked myself, and the answer lay in my schedule.

Like most of you, I was overbooked with kids, after-school activities, church life, wife life, mom life, etc. I had mistaken being busy in the church to mean that Jesus and I were splendid. I went to church twice, three times, sometimes four times a week. At that rate of attendance, I was okay, right? Wrong! I was not okay. No, not by a long shot. Just because I was present in the building, it did not mean that I was always present with the Father. Sometimes being present in church doesn't mean that we are fully engaged with the Father. Our minds wander. We cannot wait until service is over to get back to our lives. We must stop attending church because your Pastor or your mother told you to go. This behavior will not save you. We have to own why we go or why we don't go to church. You make your decision and stand by it. Go because you want to go to the Lord's house. Fellowship in the house of God brings such comfort to our souls, but it is not without friction sometimes, like everything else in life. I once read a Reddit post that said, "it was better to think of God in a bar than to think of beer in church." If you attend church, then be present and participate because anything less than that is foolish behavior.

Sincerely speaking, I was exhausted from the duties in all my roles. It seemed like I was on a runaway train with a million miles left to go. If the Lord did not stop it, I would have been on a lifetime journey to nowhere. Thank God for allowing us to have a year where we could reset the journey of our lives. Let me be clear - I am not cheering on the Coronavirus; it is a horrible virus that has devastated our lives. Instead, I am looking at the bright side of the pain. God did not leave us to drown in our schedules, conferences, and festivals. In his abundant mercy, He stepped in to save us from ourselves, and for that intervention, I am grateful. I am not saying that He caused the virus; he did not. He has given the earth to us, and it is up to us to steward it well (Ps 115:16). If we cut God out, then all the plans of the enemy succeed. However, if we cry out to God earnestly, he shows up to save us, and this is the mercy I am talking about (Is 58:6-14). There is no substitute for the presence of God. Take it from me; church activity will never equal the presence of God. Never! No amount of church attendance can change your heart for the better, especially if you don't apply kingdom principles. I had a choice to make. Either continue to act like everything was hunky-dory or confront all these issues once and for all. I chose the latter because the other way wasn't working. I had to mature in my understanding of life. Without maturity, I would be doomed to repeat my mistakes and the mistakes of others.

There is an excellent book on maturity by Peter Scazzero called *Emotionally Healthy Spirituality: It's Impossible to Be*

Spiritually Mature While Remaining Emotionally Immature. I cannot speak highly enough of the author and the contents of this book. One of the author's main points was that "pretending everything was okay was safer than honesty and vulnerability." That sentence hit home because it described me accurately. It always seemed easier to pretend than, to be honest, but God was not impressed at all. Honesty will always triumph over saving face. The book makes a compelling case for emotional maturity, for, without it, you cannot truly attain spiritual maturity.

Your heart is desperately wicked, who can know it (Jer 17:3)

I needed to take responsibility for my heart's contents and see what motivated me. I had to take a good look inside and investigate my emotions, thoughts, and state of mind. I had to get to the bottom of why I got angry when people acted a certain way. You see, it doesn't matter what people do or don't do; our response to those actions is the crux of the matter. The way I responded to situations showed maturity or lack of it. For instance, I would have road rage on my way to work; I would be livid at the other drivers going slow. It wasn't their fault. I was the one who left home late but, I would not take responsibility for my part because it is always easy to blame others.

I realized that you need to know what is in your heart in this walk of life because you will perish if you don't know. The Bible tells us that God's people are destroyed for lack of knowledge (Hosea 4:6). Knowing God's word keeps our hearts pure because it renews our minds, strengthens our inner man, and gives us wisdom. We can use that wisdom in everyday situations like road rage. In the heat of road rage, I would call other drivers names like idiots or fools. But the Word of God says in Matthew 5:22:

> "But I say to you that whoever is angry with his brother without a cause shall be in danger of judgment. And whoever says to his brother, 'Raca!' shall be in danger of the council. But whoever says, 'You fool!' shall be in danger of hell fire."

Yes, I may have been in danger of hellfire. Name-calling is not Christ-like because I was choosing death with my words; after all, death and life are in the power of the tongue (Prov 18:21). Jesus said in Matthew 12:37, "For by your words you will be justified, and by your words, you will be condemned." Our words are a creative force that we should use to build people up rather than tear them down. Unfortunately, in the heat of road rage, my words were cursing people instead of blessing them, and I am sure that displeased the Lord. I wish I can say I overcame that, but I am a work in progress. I am getting better at leaving home earlier if I can help it and keeping calm on the roads.

CHAPTER 2

NATURAL AND SPIRITUAL FUNCTIONS OF THE HEART

Our hearts are the libraries of our lives. There are records of your life's beginnings, stories about your childhood, adolescence, and adulthood. The way things were, your tears, your laughter, ups, and downs and all other moments are in there. Your heart is the essence of who you are. Before being born again, we are operating under our manual and mantra. We were the kings/queens of our castles. We did what we thought was right in our own eyes, just like the people in the book of Judges. "In those days, there was no king in Israel; everyone did what was right in his own eyes." (Judges 21:25). Then one day someone witnesses to you, and you accept Jesus Christ into your life. It is a powerful day when you answer the call to be a Christ-follower. I remember my spiritual father always used to say that God had to take the time to clean the junk out. The junk here was your old way of life. He also used to say that salvation was progressive, and it was not a one-and-done situation. Daily you must decide to follow Christ. With Christ being your Lord and Savior, you must give up control of your castle and learn how to operate your life under the counsel and guidance of the kingdom of God.

Some of us were born and raised in the church. Who is the king/queen of that castle? Authority figures in the house of God, like the five-fold Apostles, Prophets, Pastors, Teachers, and Evangelists, have a double edge sword to address. On the one hand, they are teaching these principles in their households and churches. Then, on the other hand, they are fending off the fiery darts of the enemy. Satan is a strategist who brings the heaviest battles on the Lord's front-line soldiers, like the fivefold mentioned above. That is why you see so many scandals coming from the pulpit because the enemy is working twice as hard to steal, kill and destroy their witness.

Whether you are newly saved, born and raised in the church, or have decades in this walk, God wants us to render our hearts, not our garments, continually (Joel 2:13). God can work with a willing heart. He is not mesmerized by the garments. Garments play a role in our lives, but the heart plays the ultimate role in our lives. 1 Peter 3:3-4 says, "Do not let your adornment be merely outward arranging the hair, wearing gold, or putting on fine apparel-rather let it be the hidden person of the heart, with the incorruptible beauty of a gentle and quiet spirit, which is very precious in the eyes of the Lord."The Lord's desire is for us to continually render our hearts to Him, so we continue to be clean. Jesus says in Matthew 15:11, "Not what goes into the mouth defiles a man; but what comes out of the mouth, this defiles a man." Well, what comes out of us defiles us more often than we would like to admit. Jesus is telling us to take stock of what comes out of us. When we continually sit at the Father's feet, he will wash the dirt of the day off our feet. The dirt comes from our interactions in life. But the thing is that each day has its own dirt, and the Lord wants us to get cleansed daily so that we can be fortified.

Let us take a moment and review a few functions of your physical heart. Your heart is an extraordinary muscular organ that is imperative to your life. It uses the circulatory system to supply oxygen and nutrients to the tissues while removing carbon dioxide and metabolic waste products. It is vital for living, and it is essential to keep this organ healthy because any negligence leads to strokes, clots, heart attacks, and loss of life. The human body works succinctly to keep you moving, but we must do our part: proper nutrition, exercise, and rest. You cannot tell everything that is going on internally by looking outside; this is where the health field comes in. As a medical professional myself, I can speak to running tests on body fluids, such as blood, urine, cerebral spinal fluid (CSF), peritoneal & synovial fluid, to assess your body's condition accurately. Your internal body has its own story to tell, and by examining these fluids, tissue samples, taking X-rays, Sonograms, and so forth, we get a more accurate picture of what is going on internally. The most current example is Covid-19 testing. You may show all the symptoms or be asymptomatic, but you are in limbo until you get a definitive result after testing.

Our bodies are resilient, but they face a lot of adversity from external and internal influences. External influences like environments (work, school, and home) to internal influences like diseases, genetic mutations, and bloodline disorders all strain our bodies. We know some of these triggers, but others elude us, and we are clueless about their ability to wreak havoc in our lives. Similarly, David knew some of those triggers could derail his life, and that is why he clung to the one who could help him - God. David's echoes remind us of Jeremiah's question, "The heart is deceitful above all things, and desperately wicked; Who can know it?" (Jeremiah 17:9). Who can know the depths of our hearts? God does! He knows our whole lineage from the beginning of time till the end of it. In Psalm 139, David shares how God knows everything about us, from making our beds in hell to darkness being as the light around us. So, if He knows everything about us, then He needs to take a seat in our hearts and live there indefinitely. God wants us to let go willingly and intentionally of the old man so he can mold us into mighty kingdom vessels.

We need to: "Put to death, therefore, whatever belongs to your earthly nature: sexual immorality, impurity, lust, evil desires and greed, which is idolatry. Because of these, the wrath of God is coming. You used to walk in these ways, in the life you once lived. But now, you must also rid yourselves of all such things as these: anger, rage, malice, slander, and filthy language from your lips. Do not lie to each other, since you have taken off your old self with its practices and have put on the new self, which is being renewed in knowledge in the image of its Creator" (Colossians 3:5-10).

Chapter 3

Who are the Fugitives?

Fugitive 1A: Temptation

"No temptation has overtaken you except such as is common to man; but God is faithful, who will not allow you to be tempted beyond what you are able, but with the temptation will also make a way of escape, that you may be able to bear it"
(1 Corinthians 10:13)

Temptations are a guaranteed part of the journey, and as long as we are in human flesh, they will not cease. But God has made a concession for situations like these- a way out. James 1:14 says, "But each one is tempted when he is drawn away by his own desires and enticed." This scripture hits the nail on the head. Our desires entice us, and we seldom resist them. We allow them to lead the way into dangerous situations. This fugitive is in the default category because the person in their unsaved state, yields to every desire the flesh throws at them, or they are saved but do not want to change. One of the worst temptations known to man is sexual. Those desires and urges wage a battle in our souls, but we need to keep in mind that sexual sin is a sin against our own bodies. God wants you and I to present our bodies as living sacrifices continually (Rom 12:1). However, if we are sinning against our bodies, God cannot move through us because we have unrighteous soul ties.

Therefore, we need to know our desires and weaknesses because we will be tempted at every turn. The enemy hopes to lure us into so much bondage that we will never fulfill God's plan for our individual lives. God forbid! May we have the courage to short circuit the enemy's plan by yielding our hearts to the Holy Spirit daily.

Fugitive 1B: Sexual Appetites Appeased
Before and Outside the Ring

Fornication and Adultery

*But fornication and all uncleanness or covetousness,
let it not even be named among you, as fitting for
saints." Ephesians 5:3*

Where do you go when one affair turns into two, three, four,
and so forth? At what point do you let go of fornication and
adultery? Is it the devil making you do it? God said that he
would make a way of escape then why are we not taking it.
If you keep falling into the same sins over and over, then
are you repentant of them? I remember being in fornication
mode, and I was 'saved.' In my mind, I remembered thinking
I could stop this at any time. But I did not do that. I yielded
to the rush of the bread eaten in secret. After the act, the guilt
and shame rose in me, and I could not believe it happened
again! Why did I pick up the phone or answer the door? It
is the same reason King David did not look away when he
saw Bathsheba. We were enticed and liked it.

Let's recall Proverbs 6:26, "For a prostitute can be had for
a loaf of bread, but another man's wife preys on your very

life." King David's decision to be with Bathsheba unleashed such turmoil in his house. According to 2 Samuel 12:10, 'the sword never left his house.' What a grave outcome it was, for a moment of weakness. Indeed, our actions have consequences that can be detrimental. That is why the Lord always has an escape plan for moments like these. How often do we seek it out and take it, is the question? I neither sought it out nor took it; instead, I justified my presence and told myself that this was the last time. It rarely ever is, is it?

Our flesh is vulnerable, weak, and susceptible to all kinds of suggestions. In my early days of being saved, I would try my best to fend off temptation, only to fall victim to it. It was not until I moved in with my sister from another mother where things changed. My roommate walked with such purity that it inspired me to do the same. I learned how to become accountable and vulnerable to my sister. Deep down, I knew better but having an accountability partner motivated me to do better. Now I was winning the battle of fornication, and I thank God for her all the time.

We all know things change when we change, but the honesty of the situation here is that we do not want to change. God has given us the tools to combat the flesh, but we rarely ever use them. Galatians 5:16 (TPT) says, "As you yield to the dynamic life and power of the Holy Spirit, you will abandon the cravings of your self-life." This is the problem with sexual sins. We are not yielding or choosing the power of the Holy Spirit. We have chosen our own needs over the Trinity.

Me->Father ->Son -> Holy Spirit

When it should be:

Father->Son->Holy Spirit->me

In Natasha Grbich's book *Repentance: Cleansing Your Generational Bloodline,* she ascertains that sexual sin is in all our bloodlines and, until we repent of it, it will continue to reign through the generations. That is why we are still grappling with this fugitive. We let it reign because Proverbs 9:17 says, "Stolen water is sweet, and bread eaten in secret is pleasant." It feels good in the moment and satisfies our flesh, but our spirits are tormented. So, when we are continually caught in these acts without any sign of slowing down, then the word of God becomes ineffective in our lives. As long as we are putting our sexual needs first, it does not matter how many Sundays, bible studies, and conferences we attend because our hearts are still in the default setting of self-gratification.

We can choose to change by being accountable and disciplined.

Being Accountable

Accountability goes a long way to keep you from sexual impurity, rather than surrounding yourselves with yes men and women. How about you develop friendships with people who will be brutally honest about your actions and help you through them. Perhaps a prayer warrior or two who can see the spiritual covenants that cause you to stumble and break them. These people do not have to walk on eggshells around you but can give you the truth about you head-on, and you can take it. Maybe you are being insensitive, egotistical, or have a lustful eye. Now, how are you ever going to change or overcome if you surround yourself with yes men and women? I hope you get the courage to find this kind of accountability within your circles if you haven't already. We need to be accountable even after the ring, the enemy never stops pursuing our downfall, and a ring only intensifies the pursuit. Did you know that sex before and outside of marriage gives the enemy a right to destroy your marriage bed? Potiphar's wife was a married woman, but that did not stop her from hitting on Joseph. "And it came to pass after these things that his master's wife cast longing eyes on Joseph, and she said, "Lie with me." (Gen 39:7) We all know how that story ended; Joseph loved God too much to dishonor him. However, Potiphar's wife did not regard the Ancient One nor consider his ways. She was most concerned about herself, just like how we are sometimes. This is why infidelity is still rampant and plagues many a household. Marriage resolves nothing if we do not surrender our sexuality to the Father. He has the power to dissolve those unrighteous covenants made by our disobedience. Those covenants contain curses listed in (Deuteronomy 28:16-68) and can only be dissolved if we are genuinely remorseful.

God is more than able to redeem our innocence and purity, regardless of how many sexual partners we have had.

Being Disciplined

Surrounding yourself with like-minded people in Christ shields you against this fiery dart of the enemy. You can also learn how to discipline your body by believing and declaring the word of God over it. Daily ingestion of the word of God transforms you from the inside out. There is so much power in his word to renew, strengthen and reform you. You and I just need to want him more than anything this world has to offer. We all put energy into things we think will make us better; college, exercise, eating well, etc. We know how to feed our mind and soul, but we do not know how to tell our-selves NO in places where it counts the most. Fornication, adultery, and lewd behaviors strengthen curses in your blood-line. You go in with one spirit and come out with seven more spirits attached to you. With that continued behavior over time, you have compounded interest in the sexual sin cate-gory. Now the enemy can establish his dynamic strategy to steal, kill and destroy your lineage. This is why we must fight for our sexual purity in the kingdom of God. You do not want the 'blessing' of the enemy in this area. He plays the gener-ational game, coming for you and your family even if they haven't been born yet.

For some of us, we easily give in to our desires without a fight.

It hurts my heart to see these kinds of scandals emanating from the Lord's house! What is the problem? The heart is still in the default setting and is unaffected by the word of God. In one video Jackie Hill Perry said it best when she said, "The unsaved people say, how can you expect me to believe in a God who has not been able to change you." Resisting the work of the Holy Spirit strengthens the weapons in the enemy's camp. Then our way of life testifies against us, and we become just like the Pharisees and Sadducees- hypocrites. We must fight the good fight of faith for our purity. By not fighting for our purity, we devalue our worth and crucify Jesus again. Whether you are married or not, you and I are called to live in sexual purity. Not heeding to that call with everything we have got makes us hypocrites who honor the Lord with their lips, but whose hearts are far from Him (Matt 15:8). I got tired of the hypocrisy I was living in, but I could not stop it by myself. The Lord sent me a sister who could walk with me without judging my past, and she became my keeper. I hope you have someone like that in your life.

Let us focus on relationships that didn't work out for a second. Most married couples divorce due to irreconcilable differences. This means that they could no longer see eye-to-eye or compromise in their relationship. Think of how many irreconcilable differences you have had in all your relationships. If you have had a bad breakup sometimes, you need to leave the state just to get away. We can all agree that some of our relationships are better left in the past. There is a school of thought that says you need to learn from each other in all your relationships. Even the ones that do not work out, you need to learn something about yourself from it. The problem is that some of us do not re-evaluate ourselves after a relationship ends; we just move on to the next person. We are leaving no time to heal from the wounds of the previous relationship. The door is not closed properly in that situation.

Then we take on the cycle of rebounding and relapsing into toxic relationships.

Contrary to popular opinion, marriage does not close the door to our past relationships. Nor can it heal our wounds from the past; only God can do that. Here we are broken, walking down the aisle or standing at the alter hoping that a ring can do what only God can. It can't. Open those books in your heart of past relationships and evaluate them with the Holy Spirit. With his help, we can deal with those lingering feelings and close those doors properly, so that they don't poison our current relationships. That is how some affairs happen. Doors didn't close properly, so there was a reunion when there was not supposed to be one. We must look at all our relationships through the lens of the Father. All irreconcilable differences can be reconciled with God and leave you in a better place no matter how traumatic the relationship was.

Christ-like

1 Samuel 16:7; Man looks on the outer appearance, but God looks at the heart. Jesus is the Son of God and, ergo, like Father like Son.

Matthew 5:28 says, "But I say to you that whoever looks at a woman to lust for her has already committed adultery with her in his heart." Jesus did not look at people lustfully because he kept his heart pure. A pure heart cannot be baited by Satan. Also, Jesus' love for the Father was greater than any temptation he faced. The love of God that is in our hearts purifies us and sustains us through temptations if we let it.

Questions:

How do you look at people?

What do you see when you look at people?

What are some of your weaknesses and triggers when it comes to the opposite sex?

How will you tackle this fugitive the next time it shows up?

Prayer for Single Individuals

Lord, forgive me for my sexual impurity; forgive me for not fighting the good fight of faith in this area. I ask you, Lord, to cleanse me from this fugitive and all its fruit. I renounce all covenants made by my forefathers concerning sexual immorality. I repent for joining myself with all kinds of pornography, immoral sexual acts, and seeking its pleasures in every form. I ask for the blood of Jesus to wipe away every covenant I made by (flirting, kissing, fondling, sleeping) with someone. If there was fruit, I ask you, Lord, to cleanse my child (ren) from the curse of sexual immorality. Teach me how to present my body as a living sacrifice continually. Show me how to bring holiness to each member of my body. You say that people that engage in these behaviors cannot inherit the kingdom of God. I ask for mercy in the throne of grace to help keep my sexual purity. I do not want to be disqualified from the race because of my lack of self-control. At the scent of temptation, Lord, I ask you to show me a way out and give me the strength to take it. I want to love and honor you with all of me, teach me how to do that and not sin against You and my own body. I choose you this day and take on the armor of God wherever I go. I surrender my heart to the Lordship of Jesus.

In Jesus' Name, Amen.

Prayer for Married Individuals

Lord Jesus, I repent for straying from my betrothed spouse. I ask you, Lord, to wash me and cleanse me from the fugitive of adultery. I renounce sexual immorality from my bloodline.

Lord, purge this sin and its fruit from my children's legacy so that they will not be adulterers. I pray for the child(ren) I had in my affairs, that they are cleansed and redeemed from this curse. I repent for engaging in every form of adultery (thought, word, and deed). I ask from the throne of grace that I may find mercy every time this fugitive comes in all its forms (visually, mentally, emotionally). I surrender my heart to you right now and ask for the blood of Jesus to cut ties with the spirits of adultery. I want no part of it, and I declare this day that I am one with my spouse. I ask for the healing wings of Jesus to mend my relationship with my spouse. Take me back to a place where I honored and treasured my spouse. I declare I am willing to do the work necessary to be reunited with my spouse emotionally, mentally, physically, and spir-itually. I cut the covenant I made with the enemy to deny my spouse intimacy because of bad situations. I repent for substituting intimacy with my spouse with pornography and other unrighteous sexual acts. Let me find comfort, joy, and peace in our marriage bed. May our union reflect heaven on earth, and may we be bound with bonds that cannot be broken. I surrender my heart to you, Lord. Only you can restore me and put a right spirit within me. Thank you for blessing me with an amazing spouse to live out my days. I invite you, Lord, to be the center of our union always, and when temptation knocks, I declare Jesus will open the door and curse it at its root.

In Jesus' name, Amen.

Fugitive 2: Choosing Darkness

> "Who changed the truth of God for a lie and
> worshipped and served the creature rather than
> the Creator, who is blessed forever." Amen.
> Romans 1:25

2A: The Cover-Up

One definition of a cover-up is to conceal the truth or evidence of wrongdoing. There are a thousand reasons why someone would hide the truth. Here are a few:

Shame
Guilt
What will people think?
To 'protect' someone.
I know something you do not know/secret.
Deceive someone to gain control of them.

This list is by no means extensive, but you get the picture. Cover-ups complicate our lives, and however we choose to justify it, it is still wrong. Remember the adage, 'tell the truth and shame the devil.' This adage captures truth and lies accurately. There is nothing such as a righteous lie, so no matter how bad things get, we always must be brave enough, to tell the truth. In the Garden of Eden, Adam and Eve hid from God, and they tried to cover up their nakedness. After eating the fruit, Adam and Eve's eyes were opened, and they realized they were naked. So, they sewed leaves together, covered themselves up, and hid when they heard God's voice walking in the garden (Gen 3:7-8). It makes you wonder what would have happened if they confessed their sin instead of trying to cover it up. Your guess is as good as mine. What would the Lord have done if David decided to confess his sin instead of orchestrating a grand cover-up that ended up with the death of Uriah?

Let us take a closer look at David's situation. He was tempted when he saw Bathsheba bathing and sent for her. He slept with her, and when she got pregnant, he devised a plan to cover it up. This story is loaded with lies and deceit. Can you imagine being one of the servants in the household and being witness to this adulterous situation? This must have been the hottest gossip in town. His foolish behavior did not last long because the prophet Nathan brought conviction, and David yielded to the Hand of God. The Bible tells us his punishment or the consequences of his sin,

"Now, therefore, the sword shall never depart from your house, because you have despised Me, and have taken the wife of Uriah the Hittite to be your wife'. 'Thus says the LORD: 'Behold I will raise up adversity against you from your own house; and I will take your wives before your eyes and give them to your neighbor, and he shall lie with your wives in the sight of this sun.' For you did it secretly, but I will do this thing before all Israel before the sun."
(2 Samuel 12:10-12)

The Lord was angry with David and dealt with him severely. David knew that he messed up. It must have broken his heart to see that he broke the Father's heart. God had seen David through tumultuous times and withheld no good thing from him. So, this act was a huge slap in the face for God. What a way to repay a loving Father! How many places in our lives has the Father seen us through? For some of us, there are too many to count. If you cannot find any place where the Lord has been good to you, listen to your beating heart and the fact that you have breath in your lungs. Many people desire this, but their number was up; yours is not yet, so live. Find a way to God. He will heal your wounds and bind up your broken heart (Ps 147:3). I know it is easy to blame God when things go wrong, I have been there, but the truth is we have an enemy, folks. He is the one at the helm of the chaos we suffer, not God. If we live by our mantra, the devil comes for us; if we live under the mantra of God, the devil still comes for us, but this time we have the great I Am's protection. That being said, we can never repay the finished work of the cross; it is an immeasurable gift. We honor that work by righteous living, and when we fall short, we need to be eager to confess our sins and keep moving.

David realized his treachery and did not argue or justify his sin; instead, he repented it. This is where most of us fall short; we justify our stance rather than repent of it. When we are confronted with the truth, we explain our position and defend our decisions. Rarely ever do we apologize to the person. We tell people they need to see from our perspective. The Lord despises cover-ups because they show a spectacular lack of appreciation of the cross. Jesus bore them on his back and was crucified with them. So why would we want to resurrect the sins that our Lord Jesus died for? Surely, we can love Jesus better than this.

I implore you not to cover up situations; instead, surrender them at the feet of the Father, Son, and Holy Spirit. God says in Isaiah 1:18, "Come now, and let us reason together, says the LORD, "Though your sins are like scarlet, they shall be as white as snow." In essence, the Lord is saying, let's talk about it, I am a very forgiving Father. There is nothing that you have done that I can't fix. Won't you come? You know his word has redemptive powers that can sever the yoke of sin. It will teach you how to live righteously if you let it. No matter how bad the truth looks, it is always better than a cover-up. Sometimes you get deceived into thinking that you got away with it; you didn't. The foundations of the world were created in the spirit of truth, so that's why the truth always rises to the surface- always. Think of David; if anyone could have gotten away with it, it should have been him, especially since David was the man after God's own heart (1 Sam. 13:14). In the end, the truth was revealed. You see, the enemy will take your sins and use them against you in the courts of heaven. The enemy knows two things 1) he knows how the Righteous Judge rules, and 2) he knows all flesh. He is our accuser who accuses us before the Father day and night (Rev 12:10). The enemy understands the law of the word, and he knows how the kingdom of God works. The wages of sin is death unless we repent. However, if we are stiff-necked and refuse to repent, the righteous Judge finds us guilty.

Genesis 3:14 says, [to Satan] "On your belly, you shall go, and you shall eat dust all the days of your life." Then God said to

Adam in Genesis 3:19, "In the sweat of your face you shall eat bread till you return to the ground, for out of it you were taken; for dust you are, and to dust, you shall return." The dust is your flesh, and its works are adultery, fornication, uncleanness, lasciviousness, to name a few. Satan devours dust that delights in these pleasures of the flesh.

However, the plot twist happens when we confess our sins to Jesus, that case is thrown out, and the Judge rules in our favor by forgiving our sins and redeeming us from death. These deeds were crucified with Christ so that we could share in his resurrection. When we are in Christ, we are a new creation that walks in the spirit (2 Cor 5:17, Gal 5:16-18). This means that we choose God in everything we say and do. The devil cannot devour you because you live a submitted life. He knows no matter the personal cost; you will always do the right thing.

Christ-like:

When Jesus walked the earth, he set people free with the truth of the kingdom. He taught people about a loving God who was willing to walk with them through life. Jesus showed them a Father who was faithful and just to forgive humanity's trespasses if we confessed them. Jesus lived, died, and rose again to establish the truth. It is worth living for!

Questions:

Have you noticed how hard it is for people to tell the truth in certain situations? Are you like these people?

If you have a cover-up in your life, is it worth it?

What will you do about it?

How would the Father feel about your issue?

Prayer for Cover-up

Heavenly Father, in desperation, deceit, and whatever other reason, I have covered up the truth. At the time, I thought it was the right thing to do. Now I see the flaw in my thinking. The truth is the only action that sets us free. I ask for your forgiveness in covering up the truth. I ask for the blood of Jesus to cleanse me and my lineage from this fugitive and its fruit. Teach me how to tell the truth in love, and seal me with the Holy Spirit, who will guide me through life's situations. Let your wisdom be the principal thing in my life. Teach me how to bring honor to others by always being honest, In Jesus' Name, Amen.

2B: Lying Lips.

Colossians 3:9 (NIV) says, "Do not lie to each other, since you have taken off your old self with its practices." You know cover-ups go hand in hand with lies, and the Lord hates lying lips. Jesus said that Satan was the father of lies, (Jn 8:44), so we should have nothing in common with the father of lies if we are God's children. It is a severe conflict of interest when we lie. For whatever reason why we do it, 'we are flirting with darkness,' as Pastor Jeff Knight of The Rock Church says. All the enemy needs from you is a wink and a smile, and he's in your heart. The enemy will stay there and remodel your heart with his bricks of deception. After all, that is how he caused the fall of man through deceit. I do not know who came up with the name for the bad bots in the Transformers franchise, but Decepticon is so fitting a description for the enemy. He is a deceiver and a con. Whatever he does for you is for your ultimate demise. I remember reading a Christian book years ago; I do not recall the title. The author said that it did not matter if you were saved or not; everybody hates a liar, and that is so true. At the end of the day, many of us want to know if we can trust the words flowing out of your mouth? No one is interested in deciphering truth or lies every time you speak. It is too exhausting, and your time is too valuable to be spent this way. You know Joseph suffered at the hands of lying lips twice. First, his brothers lied to their father about what happened to him. The second time was at the hands of Potiphar's wife, lying about what 'he did to her' in Genesis 39:6-23. He went to prison on account of a false witness. In the Old Testament, bearing a false witness was one of the Ten Commandments. Lying lips wreak havoc by destroying destinies and ruining lives.

'The truth doesn't cost anything but a lie will cost you everything' –Unknown/Quoteistan.com

Have you noticed how there are as many broken relationships inside the church as there are outside the church? If we, who are saved, have broken relationships, then how do we give people hope? How do we help people heal their relationships when our relationships are a mess? The church has the tools to minister reconciliation among people, but it is a tall order. What hinders the bride of Christ from applying these reconciliation tools to its members? *Fransi Van Wyk*, in her book *Godly Relationships: A Key to Sexual Fulfillment*, says that Jesus died for all our relationships. She says that one can trace every pattern in their lives, including repetitive sin, back to their relationships. Jesus died to repair our relationship with the Father but also to mend our relationships with each other. She says that our relationships influence each other, and we will not enjoy fulfilling marriages if our other relationships are in chaos. The fundamental issue is some of us do not know what healthy relationships look like. Adam and Eve were the only ones who experienced a perfect relationship in the beginning. Their life with God and each other was perfect, pure, and effortless before the fall. I suspect that it broke their hearts to see humanity fight for something that came so effortlessly before the fall- (a prosperous relationship with the Father). We have a way back to him through Jesus, and we need to start inviting Jesus into our relationships. He can restore our identity and purpose so we can be complete in Him and each other. The problem is we are only giving him a piece of our hearts, so our reformation is limited. The Lord wants us to bring all of who we are to the table; mind, will, emotions, experiences (good and bad), etc. He is the only one who can help us overcome, triumph, and live a victorious life. When your heart is totally His, reformation can be complete, the ministry of reconciliation will flow at maximum capacity. No wonder why our relationships are not as rewarding as they can be, we have surrendered little, so our reformation is limited.

Broken relationships are not reflective of the redemptive power of the cross. Often, the problem is the withholding or bending of the truth. Don't the ones we love deserve the truth? I do believe the best place to start mending our relationship is by apologizing for our actions. Nothing can soften hearts more than open and honest communication. The more sincere we are, the more authentic our relationships get. The more authentic our relationships get, the less likely we are to lie to each other.

We are a royal priesthood chosen by God (1 Pet 2:9), and our lives should exude the unity spoken about in Psalm 133. We are his mediators who are supposed to reconcile with each other and the Lord. Lying lips are not reconciled to the Father of Light but the father of lies. John 14:23 says, "If anyone loves Me, he will keep My word; and My Father will love him, and We will come to him and make Our home with him." The house that the Father, Son, and Holy Spirit build in us is made from righteous bricks. As we grow and mature in the kingdom of God, the trinity builds in us a righteous dwelling. Our obedience to God's word allows the trinity to create in us clean hearts and pure hands. (Ps 24:4) It is by no means a simple task. It is a complex exercise to walk in love daily, but it is possible through him. In time, the Lord will teach you how to speak the truth in love. He will also teach you how to bring value into your relationships with vulnerable communication. May we have the courage to walk in the Lord's ways which are void of lies, deceit, or cover-ups.

Christ-like:

Jesus is the way, the truth, and the life (John 14:6). There are no lies in Him. Jesus told the truth and lived by it. He had nothing in common with the enemy.

Questions:

What lies keep you up at night?

How can you make peace with what you know?

Why do you lie? Are you aware when lies come out your mouth?

Are you ok with the status quo of your relationships? Why or why not?

Are your broken relationships worth saving?

Prayer for Lying Lips

Lord, I ask for mercy from the throne of grace for my lying lips. You said that the father of lies has no truth in him. Lord, I want no part of Satan's legacy. I repent for telling lies about myself and others. I repent for believing in lies and walking in them. All these lies do not reflect my relationship with you. I ask you to take the coal as you did for Isaiah and cleanse my lips from this evil. I renounce the propensity to lie, especially when telling the truth may be challenging. Help me mend the damage I made in my relationships by lying. Teach me again how to honor people with the sincerity and honesty of my heart. I lay this at your feet, Jesus, and ask your Father to be my Father and not the father of lies.

In Jesus' Name, Amen.

2C: Secrets and Betrayed Trust

"Would not God search this out? For he knows the secrets of the heart" Ps 44:21.

At the pandemic's height, I remember watching a documentary on TV called 'Taken at birth.' The doctor at the center of this scandal was Dr. Hicks. He lived in a small town and created a business selling babies on the black market. He would lie to the new moms that their babies had died at birth. I was heartbroken for these babies, who were now adult men and women looking for their birth families. Some had sweet reunions, while others were not so lucky because people in their families had passed away. One part of the story was where a daughter had her stepdad exhumed because she needed to know the truth about her heritage. Her stepfather had been dead since 1978! I felt her desperation as I watched the show. It occurred to me that people are deceived into thinking that they can take their secrets to the grave. The truth was never meant to be concealed, buried, disguised, camouflaged, or bent. It will constantly be exposed whether we like it or not. Some residents in the small town knew what was going on but pled the fifth. Others thought very highly of this doctor. Either way, this story reflected how things were back in the day. History has a lot of secrets that are no longer secrets anymore. These kinds of secrets break hearts when they are exposed.

The truth shall make you free-John 8:32

As God-fearing Christians, we should not have any part of these secrets or unethical activities because they detour our walk with Jesus. Secrets cause us to lie, and we already know what the Father thinks about that. Ask for the Lord's timing and guidance when the time comes to reveal them. Keeping secrets binds you to the spirit of bondage until you expose them. There is an ancient saying that states, 'evil prevails when good men do nothing.' You can do something about it. If you stumble upon life-altering secrets, pray for wisdom and guidance on the matter. When it comes to secrets involving abuse in the home, you can pray and act. Try not to be complicit in the issue and ignore it. The current laws would indict you and charge you with a felony or misdemeanor at the very least. Remember, things that are seen were made from things that are not seen (Heb 11:3). So, what happens in our courts is a mirror of what happens in the courts of heaven. The enemy will use your secrets against you in the courts of heaven. Your secrets are his evidence against you, and this is an attempt to get God to deny your destiny.

Satan uses the letter of the law to keep us bound even when, especially when we are saved. Matthew 5:25 says, "Agree with your adversary quickly, while you are on the way with him, lest your adversary delivers you to the judge." In his eye-opening book, *Unlocking Destinies From the Courts of Heaven: Dissolving Curses That Delay and Deny Our Futures*, Robert Henderson indicates the word adversary in Greek is (G476- "antidikos/an-tid-ee-kos"), and it means one who brings a lawsuit. I mentioned this scripture earlier about Satan being our accuser (Rev 12:10). If you agree with your accuser, he has no case against you. Thus, having a repentant heart is so powerful in dismantling all the evidence against you. The enemy will accuse you even if you are not involved in a matter. For example, say you suspect abuse in a family member, coworker, friend, etc., and you are silent on the issue. Your silence is what he uses to accuse you in the courts of heaven. Bear in mind that evil prevails when good men do nothing. It's time to stop the enemy dead in his tracks. Being complicit is not an option anymore. Be the voice for the abused and rescue regardless, as my church mantra says. There are laws in place like, Mandatory Reporting to help you out if you suspect abuse of any kind in someone's life. It is up to us to bear each other's burdens because this fulfills the law of Christ (Gal 6:2).

Another prong of secrets we wrestle with is being in other people's businesses. Pastor Melinda Knight usually tells us to love our neighbor, but if we can't, we need to mind our business. How right she is! If you have itchy ears, you will be in other people's business, which may be a contentious spot for you. Proverbs 16:28 (NCV) says, "A useless person causes trouble, and a gossip ruins friendships." This hurts even more if we have betrayed our friends/spouse/family member/ coworkers' trust. People tend to confide their traumas to us, and our job is to pray for them to do and whatever else the Father wants us to do for them. These people need confidants, not gossipers. We have broken trust because we did not have the discipline to keep our mouths shut. Remember, whoever goes about slandering reveals secrets, but he who is trustworthy in spirit keeps a thing covered (Prov 11:13 ESV). God smiles on dependable saints.

In the show, mentioned above I did sympathize with the daughter who exhumed her stepdad. I felt her desperation because, in my personal life, I have had to rattle a few cages to know my biological father as well. My mother has not been forthcoming with the details, but I still need to know. They were young, and he disappeared after he found out that she was expecting me. My mom never heard from him again. Either way, his blood is coursing through my veins, and he is a part of me no matter what. I am hopeful but realistic about the chances of meeting him. It was forty-one years ago. I am sure someone knows his story. Even in his absence, the Lord provided outstanding male figures in my life. My grandfather and his sons (my uncles) were my rock growing up, and so too was my adopted dad. He picked up the mantle of being a father and loved me like his own. Now I have a spiritual father who guides me through natural and spiritual matters. God has been good to me. Dear Reader, as traumatic as your past may have been, you cannot change it. I hope you have found a way to learn from it, make peace with it and move on. Don't let those secrets define you. Let them go; God is the one who defines you.

Christ-like:

Jesus said what is done in the dark will be shouted on rooftops (Luke 12:3). He healed the whole person inside and out so they could be motivated to live righteously.

Questions:

Do you consider yourself trustworthy? Why? Why not?

What things can embarrass you when the light shines?

What secrets have you not made peace with?

Who do you need to do right by?

Have you done it?

How would people feel if they heard you talking about them?

Prayer for Secrets and Betrayed Trust

Lord God, I repent for keeping secrets that destroy lives. Lord, you know the motives of my heart, and I ask you from the throne of grace to purge my heart from life-altering secrets and betraying people's trust. Lord, you despise people that sow discord and people that slander others. Please forgive me for engaging in both. I ask for the blood of the Lamb to cleanse me from this fugitive and its fruit. I ask for wisdom and understanding so I can navigate life's situations. I welcome the power of the Holy Spirit in my life so He can guide me in all things. I repent for grieving him and leaning on my understanding. I surrender my heart to you, Lord, and I say have your way in my life. Speak through me, love through me, walk through me and use me as an instrument of righteousness as long as l live. I declare this over me and my entire lineage.

In Jesus' Name, Amen.

Fugitive 3: Pride and A Proud look

> "But he who glories, let him glory in the
> Lord. For, not he who commends himself is
> approved, but whom the Lord commends." 2
> Corinthians 10:17-18.

Pride is inherent in our flesh, and when it is present in our hearts, it manifests in a variety of ways like a proud look, conceit, vanity, and the like. As a result, I will use pride and a proud look interchangeably in this section. If you have pride, you surely will present its symptoms mentioned above. Therefore, it is little surprise that this fugitive would fall into both categories of chosen and default fugitive in our hearts. Default because it comes with the nature of the flesh and chosen because we decide to boast about achieving our goals. There is a sense of pride when we put our minds to work to create products or go to college, learn a new instrument, overcome hurdles of life, and so forth. Those accomplishments bring sweetness to our soul because there is real fruit to our hard work (Prov 13:19). The problem here is that our egos puff up once the goal is achieved, and we begin to gloat and boast. You cannot tell us anything. Humility is seldom present at such times. I believe amid our achievements; the Lord wants us to honor Him with the fruits and not ourselves.

Keep in mind that we are of great importance in the Lord's sight whether we are accomplishing things or not. Therefore, walking in love and humility, honors God, no matter the accomplishment.

The love of God esteems others and puts other people's needs first. Love does not seek its own according to 1 Corinthians 13, but pride does. One of the Hebrew words for proud is (H1343 ge'eh), meaning to be arrogant, lofty, vain. Some people boast about how handsome or beautiful they are. Why boast, I say, you have nothing to do with your appearance. We had nothing to do with our skin color or eye color, or any of the features we boast about. God is one who gave us our earthly suits, period. I am not talking about makeup, which has its place for those who so desire it. I am talking about how you were created and put together in your earthly suit. It is beyond ridiculous how people brag about things they have no control over. Sometimes as saints, we take credit for what the Lord has done through us in people's lives. We say things like we prayed and XYZ happened. It's because of me. Watch out now; we can't do anything except by the power of God. He is the one that moved through you to bless his people. One plants and one waters, but it is God who brings the increase (1 Cor 3:7). We need to examine the motives of our hearts before we speak a word in such cases. We cannot be prideful about the things God has done through us. To God be the glory, he wills and works through us, not the other way round. There is no room at the Lord's table for a conceited person, but he gives grace to the humble (Prov 3:34).

A person with a proud look is self-absorbed, and everything they do is about them, which is why the Lord resists them. Here is another reason 'a proud look' is a chosen fugitive, we rest on our laurels instead of resting and trusting in God. We think our strengths and knowledge can save us, and we lean on that understanding. (Prov 3:5). When in reality, our understanding is limited, and there is no achievement more significant than the accomplishment of conforming to the image of Christ.

My Medical Technology degree cannot save you from the generational curses, nor can it heal your broken heart. Only the name and the blood of Jesus can do that. It is the name of Jesus that saves us, not our resumes, beauty, or conquests great and small. It is the name of Jesus that breaks curses and delivers us out of the fowler's snare. It is also the name of Jesus that every knee bows to, and every tongue confesses (Phil 2:10-11). It is the name of Jesus that saved us from certain death and reconnected us back to God. He is the way, the truth, and the life (John 14:6). Paul was right; all our achievements are dung in comparison to our Lord and Savior Jesus.

Pride is the iniquity that compromised Lucifer in heaven (Ezekiel 28:15). God had to change his name and relieve him of his duties because of it. Pride boasts of its conquests, and it seeks glory from everyone. Pride runs with the spirit of control because everything must be done to the prideful one's expectation. These people typically have their way or the highway attitude, thus making them hard to work with. Look at King Nebuchadnezzar in the book of Daniel. He exalted himself and insisted on being worshipped day and night. Proverbs 16:18 says, "Pride goes before destruction, and a haughty spirit before a fall," and boy did he fall. God humbled him and brought him low. "For seven years he roamed the fields with beasts, ate grass, his hair grew like the eagles, and he had nails like bird claws." (Dan 4:28-33). Finally, after seven long years, he acknowledged the One true God and repented of his sin. King Nebuchadnezzar learned the hard way about pride; no one is greater than our God.

It is pride that turned angels into devils, and it is humility that makes men as angels-Saint Augustine.

Walking in humility and constantly thanking God is a massive antidote for this fugitive. James 4:7 says, "Therefore submit to God. Resist the devil, and he will flee from you." True humility says that it is the breath of God in me that causes me to triumph. "...It is no longer I who live, but Christ lives in me" *because* you live a humble life (Gal 2:19-21). Knowing that you and I are held in the palm of God's hand for a specific time and season should make us want to live our lives in His purposes. Tomorrow is not promised to anyone, so live with the oil lamp burning. It is God that gives us life; let us use that life for Him and not ourselves. Consider the words of Paul below when you sense pride rising up in your heart:

"God has given me the grace to speak a warning about pride. I would ask each of you to be emptied of self-promotion and not create a false image of your importance. Instead, honestly assess your worth by using God-given faith as the standard of measurement, and then you will see your actual value with an appropriate self-esteem." (Rom 12:3 TPT)

Christ-like:

For whoever exalts himself will be humbled, and he who humbles himself will be exalted- Luke 14:11. In this parable,

Jesus was encouraging us to walk in humility in this life. Pride profits nothing.

Questions:

Do you consider yourself a proud person?

Why or why not?

How do you handle your successes and failures?

How do you feel when people describe you?

Do you seek to be the center of all your relationships?

Do you feel like you take credit for the things the Lord has done through you?

Prayer for Pride and a Proud Look

Lord God, I repent for making myself more superior than others. I repent as a lineage for gloating, boasting, and tooting my own horn when it comes to my accomplishments or anything I do. Forgive me for taking credit for the things you have done through me and boasting about spiritual gifts, when it is you who has given them to me without repentance. I repent for having a stiff neck when people try to talk to me about how I make them feel. Forgive me for not bringing the ministry of reconciliation to those around me including my family, friends and neighbors. Lord, I renounce pride and a having a proud look in my lineage. I ask for the blood of Jesus to nullify that contract. I like Paul declare my accomplishments dung compared to Jesus. I repent for having lofty eyes and wholeheartedly submit to God. Teach me how to subdue my flesh and walk humbly before you. No earthly prize is worth boasting in except the power of the cross. I surrender my heart to you and ask that you sear this fugitive in me and my lineage. From this day forward, I will glorify God in everything I lay hands on. It is by your breath I live, move, and have my being; apart from you, I am nothing. Help me to realize this in all my comings and goings.

In Jesus' Name, Amen.

Fugitive 4: Ingratitude

The things you take for granted,
someone else is praying for- Online blog post.

Merriam Webster defines ingratitude as forgetfulness of or poor return for kindness received. Synonyms include thanklessness, callousness, thoughtlessness, rudeness, lack of appreciation, and consideration. Whatever descriptor, synonym, or idiom you use, this is a deplorable trait in humans, especially in the house of faith. Ingratitude is a poor posture of the heart. Some of us are blessed to be born with grateful hearts, but the rest of us need to work this out in our faith walk continually. We choose this fugitive because we think very highly of ourselves. In a way, ingratitude is pride's cousin. We think we deserve special treatment because of who we are, and we will treat you any way we please. We expect people to give us 100% all the time, but we won't allow them to expect the same from us. We are grateful only for things that meet our expectations. We judge people based upon what is given instead of being thankful for what was given. Keep in mind that it could have been nothing.

Gratitude is one of the Lord's priorities in our hearts because it gives us a great perspective in life. A grateful heart sees the hand of God no matter how dire the circumstance. This heart knows that everything works out for those who believe in Him. Psalm 50:23 (NLT) says, "But giving thanks is a sacrifice that truly honors me. If you keep to my path, I will reveal to you the salvation of God." The Lord will see us out of every situation when we have grateful hearts. You see, out of ignorance, choice, or default, there are times when we end up in the fowler's snare, i.e., we are in the hands of our enemy (Psalm 91:3, Psalms 31:15). God is a mighty deliverer who will never turn away a grateful heart. He will deliver you in due season, every single time!

Ingratitude to man is ingratitude to God.
- Samuel Ibn Naghrillah

The late French painter Alfred Agache said that saying thank you is more than good manners; it is good spiritually. As children, this is drummed into us. We are taught to say please and thank you, excuse me, etc. These habits form well-mannered people in society. If we can be honest, no one likes or appreciates an ill-mannered child. What happens when children are not taught these principles and enter adulthood? Or worse yet, they are taught these principles but discard them as they enter adulthood. We all have experiences with people like this. Being around them is like drinking curdled spoiled milk–yuck!

Paul spoke of this in Hebrews 5:12, "In fact, though by this time you ought to be teachers, you need someone to teach you the elementary truths of God's word all over again. You need milk, not solid food!"

We are the righteousness of the Lord, and we should be walking in these elementary truths like gratitude. As saints of the Most High, we have social obligations to uphold. If we, as the Lord's chosen, exhibit ingratitude, where does that leave humanity? Jesus said in Matthew 5:16, "Let your light so shine before men, that they may see your good works and glorify your Father in heaven." Ingratitude is not a good work that shines God's glory. I understand if we have a bad day, there might not be much light shining. However, if we consistently display these attributes, then we are fooling ourselves. The reformative power of the Holy Spirit is not working in us. Yes, we can attend church all day long, fast, and pray, but attendance does not transform behavior. Allowing the Holy Spirit to mature us is what transforms us. Change always happens from the inside out.

We have not been called to be thorns in people's sides but to be our brother's keeper. Therefore, to be the bearer of these qualities and profess Jesus is a sad existence. Having no manners, being ungrateful and rude, is just like drinking that spoiled milk, and who wants to drink that! Sadly, we force people to put up with us in this state because we are blessed and highly favored. Why do we deceive ourselves? You in a physical body can feed the hungry, clothe the naked, visit the sick and those bound in prison (Matt 25:36). Jesus was fully man and fully God when He walked the earth. His physical presence here was in part to show us how we should conduct ourselves as Christians. I passionately believe it matters how you treat people. It doesn't matter who you are or what title you hold; we should treat people as we treat ourselves (Luke 6:31). Showing gratitude to those around you honors God and allows the Holy Spirit to show His mercy, love, and grace through you. What an honor!

Think of gratitude as a bridge, and every time you walk it, the Lord strengthens its foundation. Now, this bridge can connect people to God, and it can withstand all kinds of weight because the Father holds up its foundation. This is not the case when you lack gratitude; no one can connect to the Father through you. This bridge is not stable, and people could lose their footing trying to cross it. Fear is its entrance, and there is uncertainty when contemplating its safety. Ungrateful people are hard to approach because you don't know if they will blow up or not. Sometimes it feels best not to approach them. Jesus is not the foundation of this bridge; the person is. One common trait ungrateful people have is that they seldom take responsibility for their actions. It is always someone else's fault. However, when things are well, they take all the credit. I pray that ungrateful people recognize the error of their ways and repent. Our world needs more grateful hearts that carry the presence of God. Hearts that have his full compassion and kindness and can make people feel loved and understood. We need Him now more than ever.

Christ-like:

Jesus was thankful for daily provisions. He fed the multitudes (Matthew 14:19). Some of His prayers were of thanksgiving. (Matthew 11:25-27, John 11:41)

Questions:

How good are you at taking responsibility for your actions?

Do you find yourself blaming others for what happened in your life? Or are people blaming you for what happened in their life? Are you willing to reconcile with them?

Do you think your trials in life are producing gratitude or ingratitude?

Are you known for gratitude in your relationships? If not, are you willing to work on this attribute for healthier relationships?

Prayer for Ingratitude

Lord God, I repent for having a heart of ingratitude, open my eyes to see the ones I have hurt with my lack of gratitude. Forgive me for being sluggish in my appreciation of people around me. I repent for harboring this fugitive, and I ask you, Lord, to cleanse me and my lineage from this spirit. It does not have a place in my heart anymore. I humbly ask you, Lord, to teach me how to be grateful and honor those around me. I surrender my heart to you Lord; use me as that bridge builder that works through kindness to show God's love to people. I submit to the power of the Holy Spirit and invite him to create in me a grateful heart that will always reveal the presence of God every day.

In Jesus' Name, Amen.

Fugitive 5: Bias within

"Man looks on the outside, but God looks at the heart."
1 Samuel 16:7

There are all kinds of biases in the world. If you lined them up, they could fill the Golden Corral buffet line. Here are a few examples; gender, race, religion, sexual preference, and orientation. Whatever the bias is, it is wrong because it causes you to judge people and write them off before giving them a chance. This is contrary to what Jesus said in Matthew 7:1, "Judge not, that you not be judged." Bias is a chosen fugitive because we deceive ourselves into thinking God loves us more because of how we look or who we are. Bias is another relative of pride. The fact is God loves his creation. No one person is better than the other; we were all dead at one point.

If you don't like something, change it.
If you can't change it, change your attitude.
-Maya Angelou

I consider myself a nonjudgmental person because all have sinned, especially me, so who am I to judge. The Lord reminded me of this story as I wrote this book, and here goes; please forgive me, reader, if you take offense here. I have since parted ways with this fugitive.

In 2015, my family and I flew back to Zimbabwe so my native family could meet my husband and eight-month-old daughter. We flew an Arabic Airline, and the experience was stellar. The staff was courteous, kind, and anticipated our every need. The cabin crew played with our daughter and brought her numerous snacks. However, there were two parts of the fourteen-hour trip that I want to confess here. When we first got on the plane before we took off, the pilot welcomed us in English and then switched to his native Arabic tongue. I have to say the words on the screen triggered memories of those Al Qaeda videos. And that sent chills down my spine.

Clearly, watching all those terrorist videos had created a file in my heart to fear the Middle East. What made matters worse was a few hours into the flight, I had to use the restroom. Lucky for me, we had aisle seats, so the restroom was two steps away from our seats. When I got up, a small line had already formed. Ahead of me were three people, a gentleman and two Muslim women. The line moved, and soon I was number two in line. After about 5 minutes, the lady came out, and I went in after her. Immediately I noticed that she did not flush the toilet; you wouldn't believe my initial thoughts...Suicide Bomber! Why else would she take so long in there and not flush? I judged her based on how she looked and the current climate of the season- Muslim terrorism. I am still here, so there was no way that that innocent woman was a terrorist. So much for not judging people, yet here I was judging the pilot and the woman because of their culture and religion. I was wrong! At that moment, when I heard the pilot speak, bias had already taken root.

Before this encounter, I didn't know that bias had taken a seat in my heart. It crept in when I was unaware and did not reveal itself until the 'incident on the plane.' Satan could have used this evidence of bias against me before the Father; remember, he is accusing us day and night (Rev 12:10). I would be held accountable for having this fugitive in my heart if I didn't repent of it. I repeat; it doesn't matter how it got there; it matters how you deal with it. So, I turned it in to the Father and asked for forgiveness. Two noteworthy things here, first, defending my bias because of 9/11 or the Middle East perpetuates stereotypes. It effectively stops the love of God from flowing in that area. Number two, my response to the presence of bias in my heart shows who is in control, Jesus or Satan. Jesus was right about being defiled, what came out of me was bias, and it had to go.

Yes, 9/11 happened, Syria, Iraq, Afghanistan, and other countries have crumbled from war and terrorism. The enemy moved in people's hearts to commit heinous crimes and continues to do so. The terrorists involved in 9/11 made everybody that looks like them pay the price. There are scores of Muslim people who face judgment because of what happened that day. They had nothing to do with it but are continually paying the price for it. I have been at the receiving end of the brush of bias because of my race and gender. It is not a good feeling, but here I was doing the same to another group of people. This was hypocrisy at its best!

Jesus said in Matthew 7:5, "Hypocrite! First, remove the plank from your own eye, and then you will see clearly to remove the speck from your brother's eye." Domestic terrorism or homegrown terrorism is the plank in our American eye. It has instilled fear in every facet of life like theatres, schools, concerts, malls, grocery stores, etc. Mass shootings were such a trend until the pandemic, but people got numb to it. Here we are again- post- pandemic back at it again with the mass shootings! Alas, God help us! I couldn't imagine for one second being in the theatre watching the Dark Knight, and someone started shooting. Nor could I imagine being at a country concert and fearing for my life. What about Sandy Hook Elementary or Stoneman Douglas High School?

Can you imagine being a parent of a child there or even being one of the teachers there? How about the Charleston Church shooting? Those people were in the house of God. It is unimaginable even to think how this happened. The fact that there are so many examples of mass shootings is heartbreaking. These individuals were not Muslim, so how could I fear a Muslim woman who didn't flush the toilet.

Let us face it, every religion, creed, race, tribe, and culture has evil apples. These people taint their societies and bring such heartache to their victims and their families. Unfortunately, the bias I had in my heart never gave the woman the benefit of the doubt. Maybe she thought she flushed; maybe she was tired of being in there and just left. Perhaps it wasn't hers, and it could be she didn't know-how. Honestly, some aircraft toilets are so confusing these days. Regardless of the reason, I never gave her the benefit of the doubt. Instead, I labeled her a terrorist and prayed to God to save us. How ironic!

The Lord knows my comings and goings. He knows when I will check out of here (earth) and how it will happen. At that moment on the plane, I was scared of dying. Like most humans, I feared death, but the real problem was if I admitted fear, where was my faith? The faith walk's conundrum is that if we say we are scared, then we have no faith.

What we should be saying to fear is, God is coming for you. Acknowledge its presence and call on Jesus to go and sit in that area of your heart. Joyce Meyer once said in one of her devotionals that God was our deliverer. She stated that we could not be delivered from something if we refuse to admit it. We will never be free from anything we keep excusing. It saddens me how many of us still wrestle with these issues inwardly but save face on the outside. When Jesus comes to sit in that struggle, he brings his name, blood, and authority to deliver you.

Bias and love cannot occupy the same space. Jesus said in Matthew 6:24, "No one can serve two masters; for either he will hate the one and love the other, or else he will be loyal to the one and despise the other." So, I had to choose, either justify my bias or let it go. The longer I defended bias, the stronger the yoke became. Once a yoke like bias strengthens, it begins to dilute your righteousness. Soon I would be like those phobic people labeling people based upon their exterior and judge them harshly for it. Saints of God, I could not let that happen. I did not let my bias dehumanize people; after all, they are people too. I gave it up to Jesus and allowed Him in his authority to occupy the area of my heart where bias had taken root.

If you find yourself having issues with a particular group of people, ask the Lord to help you shed light on why and surrender the bias to him. Bias sows discord among brethren and makes it hard to build relationships with people that are not like us or look like us. We are quick to judge them and throw scriptures at them to make our point. The human that is not like you is not your enemy. Your enemy is Satan himself, and he moves through people that allow him to do so. "For we do not wrestle against flesh and blood, but against principalities, against powers, against the ruler of the darkness of this age, against spiritual hosts of wickedness in heavenly places." (Eph 6:12) Let us make a stand and decree that we will no longer allow the enemy to move through us.

The most basic need of a human is the need to be loved. There is no better love than God's love for us. His love for us covers a multitude of sins, restores us, affirms us, defines our very existence, and brings immense unity. This is the love that is needed to heal and change the world. We do not need rock-throwers, like those in John 8:3 who were willing to kill the woman because she was caught in adultery. We, too, have been caught up in lies, adultery, fornication, curious sexual appetites, addictions, etc. This is what is wrong with some of us Christians today. We think our sins are not as bad as theirs. Saints, sin is sin. Yes, we are right about godly principles, but do we have to treat people like trash? He who is without sin among you, let him cast a stone. (John 8:7). Jesus died for them just like he died for you and me! "Judge not, that you be not judged." (Matt 7:1). Leave the judging to the Righteous Judge! Our part is to love our neighbor as ourselves no matter who our neighbor is. We don't have to agree or like their choices in life, but we have to love them. It is not for any of us to judge people in any way, but it is up to us to love and pray for each other. I have friends who have made different life choices from me, and they need my love and prayers, not my judgment. My fervent prayer is that God uses us to reach them and save them from the enemy's clutch. Judging does not lead a man to repentance; the goodness of God does that (Rom 2:4). May we be more vigilant against this fugitive. It should have no place in our hearts. Let us repent of this stance and ask the Lord to teach us how to love one another. God will be merciful to them, just like how he is merciful to you and me.

Christ-like:

Jesus died for all humanity in their variety of skin color, culture, tribe, language, dialect, tongue, beliefs, and traditions.

He hung out with everyone except the religious leaders. He showed people the goodness of God, which led to many repentant hearts.

Questions:

Do you think you are biased? Why/Why not?

Is there a particular sect of people or race you may have a problem with?

If so, why? Are your reasons justified? Are you willing to let go of your biases?

What do you think Jesus would say to you about your biases?

Prayer for Bias Within

God, I renounce bias right now in the name of Jesus. Lord God, I repent for looking down on other races, cultures, genders and judging people's choices. Lord, nothing is hidden in your sight, and I ask for exposure of this fugitive in my heart. Lord, you know the depths of my heart, and I surrender my heart for you to cut away this evil within me. You created all man, so who am I to judge and look lowly on others. Teach me how to honor others despite our differences. I may disagree on lifestyle choices but help me to love them regardless of them. Let your love abound in my heart so I can love others as myself. I choose to love others and not put them down for being different. Teach me how to pray for them and turn the other cheek when offenses happen. I declare this over me and my lineage, in Jesus' Name, Amen.

Fugitive 6: Your way is the right way.

"Go therefore and make disciples of all nations, baptizing them in the name of the Father and of the Son and of the Holy Spirit, teaching them to observe all things that I have commanded you" (Matt 28:19-20). Bible scholars and teachers call this the Great Commission. This is the mandate of the bride of Christ to baptize and teach the world the word of God. Another verse that comes to mind is the following, "A plan (motive, wise counsel) in the heart of a man is like water in a deep well, but a man of understanding draws it out" (Proverbs 20:5 AMP). So, between these two scriptures, our mandate is clear 1) baptize, teach about the kingdom, and 2) use the Lord's understanding to position people to move in their purpose. Molding people into your image instead of what the Lord wants for their lives is where we miss the mandate. Honestly, sometimes it seems like we are married to our opinions and sell them as the gospel. This is the reason why our way is a chosen fugitive. We need not be married to our way of doing life but to the unchanging word of God and its principles.

Looking back at my life, I was walking in pride, thinking that I had the answer to your problems! I have fallen into this so many times as a mentor pushing college on all my mentees.

Coming from Africa, sometimes it pains me to see wasted opportunities. If some of these opportunities were present in the motherland, they might not get wasted. I am a firm believer in education because it can enhance your skillset and better your life. I had a sweet-spirited mentee who has a fantastic personality. I saw myself in her and offered to be her mentor. We have a beautiful relationship, and, like all relationships, it has its ups and downs. You see, I wanted her to go to college and make something of herself. So, I shoved college down her throat repeatedly.

What should have happened was that I, as her mentor and intercessor, should have sought the Lord on her behalf. Honestly, I did not, because to me, college is key to a better life. I am not saying that her life was bad-it wasn't. College is what I did, so that is what she needed to do, period. Looking back on the experience, I had to apologize to her for trying to make mini-me out of her. I already exist, so why do I have to duplicate myself.

My mentee went to college for a season and decided that it wasn't for her. I wanted to drop kick her for not listening to me, and I even told her as much. I backed off her a little in my feelings, and I told her I would always be there for her. Not even a year later, she figured out what she wanted to with her life and enrolled in Massage Therapy School. She recently graduated in December 2020. Go, girl! I was so proud of her, and I finally learned what the Lord was trying to tell me. She was made in My image–not yours! The idea here is to awaken the assignment in people by constantly seeking the word of God for their lives. The blueprint of purpose is unique to every individual, and it takes the wisdom of God to draw it out. What my mentee needed was to learn who she was in the kingdom of God. She was born and raised in the church and had the most loving family. My mentee chose to go to a school that better suited her persona.

Be teachable, you're not always right–Anonymous

As humans, it is easy to fall into man-molding traps. We take people under our wings and teach them how we do things. In some cases, this mentor relationship works out, but in other cases, it doesn't. We really should be unlocking destinies for people rather than giving them our blueprint of purpose—no two people alike, no two people have the same fingerprints. Our function in life is as rare and unique as our fingerprints. So why do we strive to look the same? Society has a schedule for humanity; born-school-college-marriage-two kids-work-retire-go home to be with the Lord. It is this kind of thinking that causes us to stumble. Repeating the timelines of our lives on others is not prudent. It shows that we value our traditions more than the word of God. These traditions (habits, practices) keep curses alive and keep our lineages in bondage. The Lord's word should supersede our ideals, not fit into them! It brings heartache and sorrow when we imitate what others did in their life, in our lives, and it doesn't work.

I still believe in mentorship, even though it took me a while to understand how it should work. It is such an immeasurable and invaluable tool in various fields like sports, writing, acting, IT, dance, etc. There are visible metrics to evaluate mentees' progress, and the plan can be adaptable to the kinds of mentees you have. In such instances, your mentee's (s) assignment is at the surface. Every time you look at their faces or see them in action, you see their purpose. You don't have to dig it out. In my mentee's case, her assignment was buried deep, and I needed the wisdom of God to draw it out. I have learned my lesson; inquire of the Lord the intention of your mentees especially if their purpose is obscured. It is worth digging for. Take it from me. Try not to use your blueprint on others; it causes unnecessary heartache. Myles Munroe said it best in his book, *Applying the Kingdom: Rediscovering the Priority of God for Mankind,* "Life's greatest failure is to be successful in the wrong assignment." May we have the wisdom of God to usher people into their proper assignment instead of our assignment.

Christ-like

His blueprint is what we should be walking in.

Questions:

If you have a mentor (s), did they help you land on the right page of your life?

If you are a mentor, how successful have you been at unlocking your mentees destiny?

Do you feel that your destiny is unlocked? Why or why not? If not, what are your next steps?

Prayer for Your Way is The Right Way

Lord, I repent for pushing my ideas on others. I repent for trying to recreate myself in others. Forgive me for not digging deep and drawing out the destiny of my mentees. Teach me how to pray for them and how to draw out what you put in them. Teach me how to look at them and see them as you see them. I pray that this fugitive will not establish itself in my lineage. I renounce this fugitive and its fruit from my life.

In Jesus' Name, Amen.

Fugitive 7: Robbing Caesar, Robbing God

"Render to Caesar the things that are Caesar's
and to God the things that are God's" Mark 12:17

Let us peel back the onion of taxes for a second. The American government created taxes to help fund public goods and services like police, judiciary, Social Security, to name a few. This income helps pay for recurring and non-recurring expenses of the country. Both state and federal governments give back the excess you paid throughout the previous year during tax season. According to history books, the Civil war in 1913 led to the creation of Income Tax which grew over time. Think of it as Caesar's cut of your pay. Fast-forward a few decades, and we find ourselves as experts, taking advantage of the situation. The question is, how reliant are you on your tax refund? Are you filing righteously? If it were to go away, would you be, ok?

Robbing Caesar is a fitting example of ill-gotten gains. You are getting your 'blessing' through unrighteous means. This is not an honest way to get an income, and it shows where your heart truly lies. It lies in the manufactured system of government and not God. Ill-gotten gains are, in a sense, fruit of a poisonous tree. They compromise our walk with the Lord. Even if we were to tithe and give offerings on these gains, the Lord would not accept them. Why? Because we robbed Cesar when he told us not to (Mark 12:17). Indeed, we are not listening nor obeying his word (1 Sam 15:22).

"For where your treasure is, there your heart will also be." Matt 6:21

If our hearts are more willing to deceive the system than follow God, we are, in essence, half dependent on God and mammon! The walk of faith is supposed to be entirely reliant on God. His hand was swift to provide food and water in the desert every day for the Israelites.

> "Then the Lord said to Moses, "Behold, I will rain bread from heaven for you. And the people shall go out and gather a certain quota every day, that I may test them, whether they will walk in My law or not. And it shall be on the sixth day that they shall prepare what they bring in, and it shall be twice as much as they gather daily." (Ex. 16:4-6)

He fed Elijah in the wilderness through ravens "And it will be that you shall drink from the brook, and I have commanded the ravens to feed you there" (1 Kings 17:4). The

Bible is full of examples of how the Lord has provided for his people. Just as God provided a ram as a substitute for Isaac in Genesis 22:12-14, He also provided His son Jesus as the ultimate sacrifice. If our God can provide for them, he can surely provide for us. I get it, sometimes believing that your bills will be paid on time without money in the bank is a stretch of faith. But we need to learn to trust Him. Finances are sticky because some of us do not have good spending habits. We do not steward our money well. The best thing here is to learn how to steward our money. There are so many resources available to make us more competent in our finances. Then we can take those finances and tithe on them and give offerings. The Lord blesses someone who understands the principles of tithing and offering. Keep in mind Malachi 3: 10, "Bring all the tithes into the storehouse, that there may be food in My house, and try Me now in this," says the LORD of hosts, "If I will not open for you the windows of heaven And pour out for you such blessing That there will not be room enough to receive it."

"Will a man rob God?"
Malachi 3:8

When you give to God, it comes back to you. His way is full of provisions in every area of your life. It goes beyond food and clothes and gives you hope and peace in this life. Only if we are obedient to his voice. David said this, "I have been young, and now am old; yet have I not seen the righteous forsaken, nor his seed begging bread." (Ps 37:25). If he can take care of the sparrows that neither toil nor spin, according to Matthew 6:28. He surely can and will take care of you, me, and ours because we are His!

Some of us need a reality check when it comes to finances. Just as we need to resist temptation in our bodies, we should resist the urge to overspend. We will not take care of ourselves, let alone someone else if we lack discipline and accountability in this area. We spend our most valuable resource (time) working. Therefore, we need to learn how to spend it wisely and not be slaves to it. Dave Ramsey has a 13-week course on Financial Peace which our church body took back in 2007. We learned so much about finances. One of Dave Ramsey's favorite quotes was, 'sell everything and make the kids think they're next.' He was saying that once you have your eye on the prize, run with gazelle intensity. Make your budget, cut out all the extra, and focus on your goals. We cannot continue to cheat the system. How about we invite God into this area of our lives for total transformation. He is our source, not the government.

Let us consider the words of Jesus in Matthew 6:31-34, "Therefore do not worry, saying, 'What shall we eat?' or 'What shall we drink?' or 'What shall we wear?' For after all these things, the Gentiles seek. For your heavenly Father knows that you need all these things. But seek first the kingdom of God and His righteousness, and all these things shall be added to you. Therefore, do not worry about tomorrow, for tomorrow will worry about its own things. Sufficient for the day is its own trouble." Therefore, saints, let us take him up on his offer and wholeheartedly seek his kingdom first. God is more than able to provide for all our needs.

Christ-like:

Jesus said to give to Caesar what belonged to him; obviously, he never robbed Caesar.

Questions:

If Jesus was physically here, would He have reason to over-turn some tables?

Have you robbed Caesar? Why did you do it?

How do you think the Lord wants you to handle your taxes and finances from now on?

Prayer for Robbing Caesar Robbing God

Lord, I repent for having poor money habits. Lord God, I repent for me and my lineage for making the government our savior. I repent for these ill-gotten gains, and I ask you, Lord, in the throne of grace, to have mercy on me. Teach me how to apply your wisdom in my financial situations. I declare that the Holy Spirit will guide me to the right resources that will help me manage my money. I declare that my treasure is in you, Jesus, and not in Caesar. I surrender my heart to you, Lord. Teach me how to seek the kingdom of God first before I seek my own. This day my lineage and I renounce cheating the system for personal gain. We will no longer pursue ill-gotten gains, but we will pursue the King and his kingdom. Thank you, Lord, for the wisdom and discipline concerning my finances.

In Jesus' Name, Amen.

CHAPTER 4

WHAT IS YOUR HEART REALLY SAYING?

"For as he thinks in his heart, so is he." Proverbs 23:7

It is essential to examine our thoughts because they reveal our internal state of mind. Our inner man, if you will, manifests in our emotions, words, and how we treat people. Let us talk about emotions. They are not a bad thing, even though in some circles, they get a bad rap. Back in February 2019, our dance team was invited to Costa Rica to hold dance workshops. Dr. Patti Amsden was one of the main speakers there. One morning I sat next to her for breakfast, and we started chatting about emotions. I will never forget how she described them. She said, "emotions are the thermostat of your life." I was blown away by that analogy.

The thermostat is temperature- controlled. The temperature has to be at the right degree for the heat or cool air to kick on. That is precisely how our emotions work. Some conditions cause you to explode in anger or erupt in joy. While others make you cry and weep. Whatever the emotion is, it is telling you what your heart is saying at any given moment. You have to work through them to see why you respond the way you do. Often, how you feel about something tells you how far you have come or how far you have to go to resolve it. Remember my road rage story. Working through the anger revealed that I was immature when it came to handling road rage. I had to acknowledge that before I could fix it. We cannot mute or ignore them any longer. Not acknowledging emotions makes us less human and hardens our hearts. We harden our hearts because we do not want to feel the pain anymore. Life has dealt a cruel hand for some of us, and it seems easier to 'forget' the pain rather than deal with it. The reality is we don't forget; we ignore it and pretend that it didn't happen. No one has ever been healed or delivered by ignoring their pain. Like I said earlier, we have to open those books with the loving Father so he can heal us. Or we will make the wrong people pay for a pain that they did not cause.

I admire people who have overcome their traumas and make it their mission to help others. Think about the victims of

PTSD, drug, sex, mental and physical abuse who have over-come their traumas. This means that they have defeated their demons and are helping others slay theirs. They can go in and out of those memories without a second thought. The door to their past has transformed into a bridge that others can use. It is not so with some of us who will not even acknowledge what happened. Even the Lord is banned from that trauma.

Like most of you, I have repressed painful memories from my childhood and teenage years. I was not treated well in some cases, but in other cases, the opposite was true. There is one particular story I will share with you about letting God in on my pain. I was so skinny and flat- chested sometimes people would make fun of me. Even strangers would make comments about my appearance. When I was eighteen, I got a job at a local pizza store called Pizza Inn, and I worked the register. One day my high school crush came in to buy pizza with his friends, and one of his friends started making fun of me.

I remember his words. He said, "Wow, how come she doesn't have breasts! What happened to her breasts, where they cut off or something"? At that moment, my heart sank, but I had a job to do so; I kept smiling and continued to take their order. My high school crush told him off and asked me out. I politely declined because we both knew what he was trying to do. I was cute, and I had my choice of boyfriends in high school. They did not seem to mind my appearance. This guy was one of the few people who minded my appearance, but I had met people like that before. Deep down, I knew that I was worth my salt, but it still hurt whenever I heard myself being described that way.

My example may not be as traumatic as yours, but it was still disheartening. This boy was moving out of what he saw, as we all sometimes do. When the Lord said it was time to deal with that situation, He reminded me of instances where I hurt others with my words and deeds. Now, we all can recall situations where we have injured others with our words. Therefore, if God had forgiven me, who was I to withhold forgiveness from this young man? No one is perfect, and we all make mistakes, some more grave than others, but God still forgives us. Thus, we need to pay it forward by forgiving others. Hopefully, some of us will get the courage to get the help we need to heal from the past and its trauma. Once healing takes place in your heart, your demeanor changes, and your words become seasoned with the love of God. Your treatment of others softens because you carry great compassion in your heart. The love of God flows through you without the hindrance of past pain or trauma. Matthew

12:36-3 (MSG) states, "It is your heart, not the dictionary, that gives meaning to your words. A good person produces good deeds and words season after season. An evil person is a blight on the orchard. Let me tell you something: Every one of these careless words will come back to haunt you. There will be a time of Reckoning. Words are powerful; take them seriously. Words can be your salvation. Words can also be your damnation ."

In 2011 I took a prayer course with the Eagles International Training Institute (EITI) with Minster Kim Bacon. In one of her classes, she made a profound statement, she said, 'The blessings of God are voice-activated.' If you have breath in your lungs, you can change your life for (better or worse) by the words you say. As I mentioned earlier, words can build or destroy your identity, image, vision, and purpose. That is why the Lord's spoken word can bring the most extraordinary transformation in our lives if we let it. We can use it to uproot, tear down, destroy, and overthrow word curses in our lives (Jer 1:10). Think of curses as words that are contrary to who you are in Him. But God's word is so powerful to dismantle every plot against us!

Remember everything happened when God spoke, He said let there be, and it was (Gen1:1). He gave us the same creative ability as Christians. We can shift and change the atmosphere with the power of our words. Indeed, death and life are in the power of the tongue (Prov 18:21). Therefore, if we are broken on the inside, we will create chaos with our words. Right now, our world is a bit chaotic, but if we let the word of God renew us on the inside, we could change the world. The Lord is near to us with healing and everything else we need. If we let him into our hearts fully, he is more than able to heal our hearts. A healed heart speaks words that are bathed in love and refresh the soul. It also loves without limitation and manifests the love that covers a multitude of sin (1Pet 4:8). With this kind of heart your words match your actions. There is no hypocrisy here because your lips and your heart are close to the Father (Matt 15:18). You love your neighbor as yourself because you are whole in Him (Mark 12:30). All your struggles or wrestles are settled in Him because He has established you (2 Cor 1:21). You are at peace with yourself because the peace giver is dwelling in you and that is a great place to be saints!

CHAPTER 5

THOUGHTS ON JESUS

Why we are supposed to be conforming to His image because like you, He was;

Hated: "If the world hates you, you know it hated Me before it hated you." (John 15:18) Despite the hatred of the world, He still died for humanity. How much more should we be willing to sacrifice?

Betrayed: "But behold, the hand of My betrayer is with Me on the table." (Luke 22:21) Even though he knew Judas would betray Him, Jesus did not treat Judas differently from the others.

Rejected: "The stone which the builders rejected has become our chief cornerstone." (Mark 12:10). Remember, the crowds he ministered to were some of the same people that yelled Crucify Him! Despite being rejected, He was and still is important and the cornerstone of our Christian faith!

Offended People: "You have let go of the commands of God and are holding on to the human traditions of men." And he continued, "You have a fine way of setting aside the commands of God in order to observe your own traditions!" (Mark 7:8-9, NIV) It is easy to forget God's commands so we can fit in with the world. We must be willing to stand up for what is right. The truth offends many people, but it is still the truth!

Not Believed: "He came to His own, and His own did not receive Him." (John 1:11). How many times have you shared something with those close to you – family or friends? How many times have they ignored you? Jesus went through the same thing. In the face of disbelief – from those closest to Him – He still pressed on and fulfilled his calling in this world.

Doubted: Then he said to Thomas, "Put your finger here; see my hands. Reach out your hand and put it into my side. Stop doubting and believe" (John 20:27, NIV). We will be doubted. People will doubt our calling, prophetic words, revelations of Jesus, or our dreams, but we must stay the course.

Plot to kill Him: John 11:48-50 the resurrection of Lazarus was the trigger for the plot to take Jesus out. Some of us have uncovered plots from people wanting our demise. It is God that stopped them in their tracks so that no harm would come to you. I declare you will not go before your appointed time.

Crucified: Matthew 27:50 "And when Jesus had cried out again in a loud, voice, he gave up his spirit." (NIV) He died for our sins. He took the punishment for our sins once and for all. You may have family members that have gone before you. Rest assured, they are your cloud of witnesses mentioned in Hebrews 12:2. It was in the script that Jesus would be crucified, and it is in our script to die at the appointed time. However, when that time comes, we will be with Him in heaven.

Jesus wants us to simulate this scripture as our way of life; anything less than this will not produce Christ's image.

"But I say to you, love your enemies, bless those who curse you, do good to those who hate you, and pray for those who spitefully use you and persecute you, [45] that you may be sons of your Father in heaven; for He makes His sun rise on the evil and on the good, and sends rain on the just and on the unjust. [46] For if you love those who love you, what rewards have you? Do not even the tax collectors do the same? [47] And if you greet your brethren only, what do you do more than others? Do not even the tax collectors do so? [48] Therefore, you shall be perfect, just as your Father in heaven is perfect." Matthew 5:44-48

He did this, so we can too! Whatever persecution we face, Jesus has faced it too, but it did not stop him from pursuing the will of God. May we be bold and brave enough to pursue the Father no matter the persecution! This is what it means to conform us to the image of Christ: not letting life's situations alter your walk and destiny in God. Afterall this earthly life is temporary. Our inheritance is eternal in Him (Rev 21:7).

CHAPTER 6

WHAT NOW?

**Kick the fugitives out by changing
the settings in your heart!**

*Therefore, submit to God. Resist the devil and he
will flee from you–James 4:7*

Step 1: Be Honest!

You do not know the level of secret sin in your life no matter how long you have been in the kingdom business. In Psalm 19:12 (NLT), David said, "How can I know all the sins lurking in my heart? Cleanse me from these hidden faults." Who knows what triggered this soul-searching prayer? Was it when he was being hunted by Saul, or was this during the Bathsheba incident? Whatever it was, it made David realize how bad the condition of his heart was! In desperation, he cried out to a faithful God who is always reliable in forgiving us. All we have to do is confess (John 1:9).

Let us try to be 100% honest about what we are experiencing in our hearts. Recall the lying lips fugitive in Chapter 2; I mentioned how open and honest communication builds authentic relationships. It all starts with you being honest in your heart with the Father. If you and I admit our deepest feelings, no matter how ugly, to the Father, he can make those crooked places straight (Is 24:2). Then, you will be straight with yourself, the Father, and humanity. It all begins with that first step of true vulnerability in Him. If you have been walking this path, then retake the step and see where it lands. There is always more to be discovered in places you thought you overcame. Suffice it to say that all this is done whenever you are ready.

Step 2: Choose Life

Deuteronomy 30:19 says, "I call heaven and earth as witnesses today against you that I have set before you, life and death, blessing and cursing; therefore, choose life, that both you and your descendants may live." The Lord tells us what to choose because our flesh is weak. It will continually choose darkness over righteousness. That is why we have to be born again. This conscious declaration before heaven and earth shifts you from the kingdom of darkness into the kingdom of heaven. Once you switch allegiance, God begins to transform you by washing you with the blood of his son, feeding you with his word, and guiding you with the power of the Holy Spirit. Jude 20 states that praying in the Spirit edifies our most holy faith. That secret weapon of praying in tongues strengthens the hidden man of heart. What is in us drives us, so let that drive be through the unction of the Spirit than the fickle desires of our flesh.

Walking with the Holy Spirit helps grow and mature the fruits of love, joy, peace, longsuffering, kindness, goodness, faithfulness, gentleness, and self-control (Gal 5:22). These fruits will strengthen and edify those around you and help you escape the temptations of life. They also possess unlimited power to quench all kinds of fugitives and cause you to hunger and thirst for righteousness (Matt 5:6).

What is our problem then? Well, here it is, we have accepted Jesus as our Lord and Savior, we pray and read our word, but we mute the Holy Spirit. We can only attain real victory if we let them work as a trio. We cannot pick and choose what to obey. We have to walk in all scripture, not just the parts we like. Say you got into a fight with a loved one, and the Holy Spirit tells you to apologize, but you refuse. You are grieving the Holy Spirit because you are not choosing life. Proverbs 15:1 says, "A soft answer turns away wrath, but a harsh word stirs up anger." Rather than mend the rift, you would rather walk away. The ministry of reconciliation cannot be fulfilled in your relationships. What a tragedy! Again, I ask, how can God be seen if you and I have broken relationships? We should be choosing life by apologizing and bringing healing to the ones we hurt.

Here is a two in one kingdom strategy that will help you choose life; continually feast on the word of God and apply its precepts. It is not enough to just read it because, even the enemy knows scripture. The application of the word with the wisdom of the Holy Spirit brings success in all situations of your life. It may not always be tangible success, but there will always be a peace that transcends all understanding (Phil 4:7). In this life, we are continually bombarded to make decisions great and small. We do not have to make them by ourselves folks, consult the heavenly host in the decisions we make. God already knows all of our tomorrows so why not go at life his way. I know sometimes we wish we could choose without consequences, but that life does not exist. We have to accept the fact that all our choices have consequences- good and bad. In that light, let us choose God, choose life, and do the right thing. That's how he intended for us to live in the first place-in Him.

Step 3: Take Responsibility

As we briefly discussed in Fugitive 4: Ingratitude, people that are ungrateful dislike taking responsibility. However, as sons and daughters of the Lord, we have to mature and take responsibility for our actions. No one will do it for us. Let's take a second look at David's situation with Bathsheba. David immediately repented his sin after God confronted him through Nathan. This is one of the many reasons God loved David. We all know that he was a mighty warrior in battle who loved the Lord with all his heart. Then, in the face of sin, he repented quickly and accepted God's punishment without any qualms. This is the kind of righteousness God is looking for, confess your sins and accept God's punishment. Hebrews 12:7-8, "If you endure chastening, God deals with you as sons; for what son is there whom a father does not chasten? But if you are without chastening of which all have become partakers, then you are illegitimate and not sons." To chasten means to discipline, to correct by punishment, refine (Merriam- Webster). Say it with me; I'm going to make mistakes, lots of them. This is what makes us human. We need to learn from these mistakes, and if they contradict His will, confess them and accept the punishment. He punishes those He loves. I know it sounds incredibly uncomfortable, but we will fall short in our maturity if we do not learn how to accept punishment. Immature people cannot be faithful stewards in God's kingdom (1 Cor 4:2).

My spiritual mother has one of the purest hearts I know. She is so quick to apologize for any misunderstandings. I am sure the Lord delights in a soft and pliable heart like hers. If it is possible, let us not cover up our sins and transgressions because everything is naked before the eyes of God, and nothing is hidden from Him. Psalm 94:9 says, "He who planted the ear, shall he not hear? He who formed the eye, shall He not see?"

Not taking responsibility means that we cannot be chastened. Then the sins remain in our lineage. Proverbs 28:13(ESV) declares, "Whoever conceals his transgressions will not prosper, but he who confesses and forsakes them will obtain mercy" In this physical body, we will always need the grace and mercy of God. Dr. Ron Horner says in his powerful book, *Overcoming Verdicts from the Courts of Hell*, sin has no expiration date! So let us choose to be brave and give it one. Expiring sin means allowing the Holy Spirit to bring up your past, and you repent for it instead of justifying your actions. Here is an example the Lord gave me: Remember the story of Ruby Bridges and her brave year at the newly desegregated school-William Frantz Elementary in Louisiana. Those opposed to the desegregation were from different age groups; some were children. If one of those children were to apologize to her now, 60 years after the event, that would stop the curse of racism in their family. Without repentance, the enemy still has a right to perpetuate racism in the bloodline for years to come. Repenting for the sins of our fathers and forefathers also expires sin. At the beginning of the book, I mentioned that some struggles are compliments of your predecessors. Well, you probably were not the one hurling insults at Ruby Bridges; it could have been your great grandfather. It doesn't matter who is guilty. You can stand in the gap and expire that fugitive because 1) the Holy Spirit revealed its presence in your bloodline, and 2) Lord has given you authority through Christ Jesus to cast it out (Mark 16:17). I am from Africa, so you can only imagine the things my ancestors were into. There is no shame in repenting for sin, especially the ones that make you feel uncomfortable. Chances are that our ancestors can't even light a candle to the people in the Old Testament, i.e., Sodom and Gomorrah. They engaged in every form of wickedness like incest, bestiality, crazy ritual sacrifices, and so on. These people were so depraved they wanted to sleep with Lot's visitors- the angels. They tried to force their way into Lot's house and take 'the men by force' (Gen 19: 3-9). The angels had to strike the city's men with blindness so they would not find the door. How crazy is that saints? Clearly, they had to go! The enemy is counting on your discomfort not to repent. I say surprise him and repent. This move will cut the head of the snake off. It will not rise again in your bloodline.

Recall the trifecta effect from earlier in the book of sin, iniquity, and transgression. We will discuss them now. Sin, as defined by current pastors and teachers of the word, means to miss the mark. In Hebrew, sin is (H2401-chata'ah), indicating an offense, habitual sinfulness, and punishment of sin. Iniquity in Hebrew (H5771- 'Aw-vone') is moral evil, perversity, depravity, guilt, or punishment of iniquity. Another definition of iniquity is the sins of the father. Finally, transgression in Hebrew is (H6588 – Pe'-she), which means rebellion against God, nations, and individuals. Transgression is also a willful intention to disobey God and his statutes. David said it best in Psalm 32:5, "I acknowledged my sin to You, and my iniquity I have not hidden. I said, I will confess my transgressions to the LORD, And You forgave the iniquity of my sin. Selah" He understood the importance of confessing all three (sin, iniquity, and transgression) because, in reality, we may not be aware of which of the trifecta caused us to fall. Don't take any chances, just repent for all of it.

> "Now the Lord descended in the cloud and stood with him there and proclaimed the name of the LORD. And the LORD passed before him and proclaimed, "The LORD, the LORD God, merciful and gracious, longsuffering, and abounding in goodness and truth, keeping mercy for thousands, forgiving iniquity and transgression and sin, by no means clearing the guilty, visiting the iniquity of the fathers upon the children and the children's children to the third and the fourth generation." (Exodus 34: 5-7)

In light of this scripture, we should be more vigilant in surrendering all our sin, iniquity, and transgression to the Father. It is our responsibility as Christ-followers to break the curses in our families by repentance so we can fulfill the purpose of why we are here. Another noteworthy point here is that the enemy learned from God about blessings. Some of us have profited by having these fugitives in our hearts. I mentioned earlier that cheating on taxes was ill- gotten gains, and so is lying to someone to gain control of them, just to mention a couple examples of this. We can go through the courts of heaven and give them back. I attended a conference in Atlanta, Georgia, with my sister back in April of 2017. The guest speakers were Apostle Robert Henderson and Beverly Watkins. During one part of the session, they mentioned that you can give back ill-gotten gains. First, you repent for your sins, iniquities, and transgressions, then you tell the Lord that you give back any gains you received by unrighteous means. We see an example of this in Luke 19: 8, which says, "Then Zacchaeus stood and said to the Lord, "Look, Lord, I give half of my goods to the poor; and if I have taken anything from anyone by false accusation, I restore fourfold."

Obviously, some of us may not be able to physically give back our gains from Uncle Sam or whomever we beguiled. But you can declare that you will no longer accept that gain and mean it. The Lord will sever that tie, and the curse stops there, in essence, expiring the sin. It is vital we mature in our faith walk and be responsible for our walk- in Jesus. As we show our responsibility, God opens doors to stewardship. More will be entrusted to you because you are mature. The MSG version of Hebrews 6:1-3 says, "So come on, let's leave the preschool finger-painting exercises on Christ and get on with the grand work of art. Grow up in Christ. The basic foundational truths are in place: turning your back on "salvation by self-help" and turning in trust toward God; baptismal instructions; laying on of hands; the resurrection of the dead; eternal judgment. God helping us, we'll stay true to all that. But there's so much more. Let's get on with it." Indeed, let us get on with maturing in the kingdom of God! True maturity in the kingdom of God brings great rewards.

Step 4: Don't leave your gifts at the church!

Your gifts are given without repentance, meaning you can use them for Him, the world, yourself, or not at all. It is your choice. No matter how evil the world gets, there is a piece of righteousness inside of all of us that shines his light. Darkness can never overcome the light, so we need to keep the light shining no matter the situation. These gifts were given to us to minister and encourage one another in the walk of faith. Often, we may not be privy to what someone may be going through, but if we continually use these gifts, we will lift the heavy burdens of others. We are a body fitly joined together, and if we use our gifts for His glory, it will edify the church. These are the gifts from the Father in Romans12:6-8,

> *"Having then gifts differing according to the grace that is given to us, let us use them: if prophecy, let us prophesy in proportion to our faith; or ministry, let us use it in our ministering; he who teaches,*

in teaching; he who exhorts, in exhortation; he who
gives, with liberality; he who leads, with diligence;
he who shows mercy, with cheerfulness."

In conjunction with the Father's gifts, the fruits of the spirit are vital to our victory in the kingdom of God. As stated earlier in Chapter 6, the Holy Spirit strengthens and edifies you. If you let him lead you, he will intercede on your behalf with groanings that cannot be uttered (Rom 8:26). You know for the multitude of spirits the kingdom of darkness has, not even one of them can overcome the Holy Spirit. His power is unmatched and is mighty to dismantle all weapons of the enemy. We can all agree, our flesh can be uncontrollable at times, but if we learn how to walk with the Holy Spirit, he will help us escape the lusts of the flesh. My prayer for you and me is that we continue to tap into his fullness and live in his guidance.

The gifts of Jesus are his salvation, name, blood, authority, and victory. We have been talking about why the enemy came in John 10:10 (TPT), but Jesus said he came to give us everything in abundance, more than we expect; life in its fullness until you overflow! Indeed, we are blessed saints of God. Now, whatever your gift is, use it every day. Just waiting to pray, worship, prophesy on Sunday is a farce. The enemy does not wait until your Sabbath day to attack you. He attacks 24/7, 365, or 366 days of the year. Therefore, we need to be vigilant and fight that good fight of faith day in and day out with the gifts the Lord has given us. Every minute of every day, the enemy is gathering data and strategizing how to take you out. 1 Peter 5:8 says, "Be alert and of sober mind. Your enemy, the devil, prowls around like a roaring lion looking for someone to devour." You cannot be devoured if you walk with Jesus. Between Elohim, Jesus, and the Holy Spirit in your life, they will see to it that no weapon formed against you will prosper 24/7, 365, or 366 days of the year!

Step 5: Give God Your Best Shot

Paul encouraged us to run as if to win the prize. The days we live in resemble what Paul talked about in 2 Timothy 3, 'Perilous times will come, people are lovers of themselves, no natural affection, and so forth.' Our lives have been filled with so many things that vie for our attention. It would seem like we are not running to win the prize of Him. Prioritizing our relationship with the Father has become near impossible. How about we try to reconnect in a new way with the Father. Let us choose Him over the excessive surfing of social media pages. We don't need to be on those sites all the time. Maybe exchange that emptiness of online scrolling for time in Him.

Declare a fast and refrain from social media every so often. You know anytime given to God is never wasted, even if it's only a moment. The other day the Lord told me that He has hidden prayer in every breath we take. That is why you can be saved with your last breath even if you lived a life without him. Nonetheless, he is not too far from us if we seek with a diligent heart. Hebrews 12:1 (TPT) says,

> "As for us, we have all of these great witnesses who encircle us like clouds. So, we must let go of every wound that has pierced us and the sin we so easily fall into. Then we will be able to run life's marathon race with passion and determination, for the path has been already marked out before us."

Indeed, the marathon is in motion as you live and breathe. The Lord wants you to run life's marathon unhindered by the snares of the enemy. You and I cannot focus on our ordained paths if we still harbor these fugitives. They weigh us down and cripple our walk with Jesus. No man can run a race carrying chains. Yet here we are! If you so desire, your next step could be to identify and evict these fugitives by the authority you have in Christ Jesus. Every eviction of each fugitive means more of Jesus in your heart. You may not want to attack them all at once but start the process anyhow. Consider starting with one fugitive, then the next, and so forth. Soon you will be transformed into the full image of Christ. Bearing the image of Christ means not letting life's situations alter your walk and destiny in God. You will be the manifest presence of God on the earth.

Finally, Brethren

You don't have to be alone in this walk; God is here. He wants to share your life with you. Whatever is going on in your life, God wants to be a part of it. He is the undefeated Creator of Heaven and Earth who gave it all just for you and me. Now it's our turn to give our all to Him. He will create in you a clean heart, set your feet on solid ground (Ps 51:10, Ps 40:2). He will watch over you all the days of your life and order your steps (Ps 121:1, Ps 133:133). Though you may stumble and fall, he will be there to pick you up over and over again.

What say you to this? Won't you give God a sincere chance of being the author and finisher of your story? (Heb 12:2) He is the One who created you and set you in the earth for such a time as this (Es 4:14). It does not matter what you have done or where you have been; what matters is now. Matthew

West has a song that asks a great question, "What if we give everything, instead of going through motions?". What if?

Whether you have been saved for a lifetime or not, let us dedicate and rededicate our lives to the One who holds it all. It is not easy living for Jesus, especially these days, but he is more than worth it. Let us allow him total access to our hearts without limitations. A real relationship with Jesus is rich in reward and fills our lives with purpose. Remember brethren; it is in the trials of life where our faith in him grows. The testimony from these seasons gives us great hope and encouragement while overcoming the powers of hell. For it is by our testimony and the blood of the lamb that we pulverize the enemy (Rev 12:11). Let us strive to give him everything because there is no better place to live than in the presence of the One who created you!

Closing Prayers

Depending upon where you are in your walk with the Lord, Jesus Christ, I've included a prayer for you below.

If you don't know or have a relationship with Jesus, please pray the following prayer,

God,

I don't know you, but I want to. I know that I am a sinner, but I want to change. I repent for my sins, iniquities, and transgressions. If there have been any ill-gotten gains from my fugitives, I give them back in the name of Jesus. I renounce every unrighteous covenant in my bloodline. Any part of me that Satan lays claim, Lord, I surrender it to you. I declare that I and my kin do not want any part of Satan's inheritance. I choose you, Lord, and I give you my whole heart Lord. Teach me how to live in your will. Teach me how to love others even when we disagree. Teach me how to not give up when the storms of life arise. I cut ties with the following fugitives (X,Y,Z). I ask for your wisdom and fortitude not to resurrect these fugitives in my heart again. Please show me where I can attend a church to be planted and grow in your word. Teach me how not to give up when things get tough in the church. Show me who I am in you and when I forget Lord, please remind me. Help me not to stray from your presence. I surrender my heart now, and I ask that you, Jesus, and the Holy Spirit come and live in my heart. Fill my heart with all of who you are. I am yours now and forever in Jesus' Name Amen.

For those who currently have a relationship with the Lord, Jesus Christ and you need to recommit your life,

Lord God,

I have lost my way; I have forgotten the lover of my soul. Lord, I repent for hosting these fugitives in my heart. I know I was bought with a price, and I am sorry for minimizing Jesus in my life. Please forgive me for turning my back on you and loving myself more than you. I repent for the ill-gotten gains these fugitives have brought, and I give them back in the name of Jesus. I ask you, Lord, to create in me a clean heart and renew a right spirit within me. I want to live for you again. I want to be on fire for you. Lord, I ask that you give me an 'unbaitable' heart. A heart that will not get baited by the enemy's vices. I ask from the throne of grace that you cut those ties that Satan has to me and my kin. I renounce and sever those covenants in the name of Jesus. Father, you said if we believe in Jesus, me and my household will be saved. I speak this over my life right now. I ask that you reveal once again your purpose for my life and let me not stray from it again. Lord, I give you access to my heart, and I yield to the power of the Holy Spirit. I rededicate my life to you again. I am yours, Lord, now and forever. I declare as Joshua did that, me and my house will serve the Lord.

In Jesus' Name,

Amen.

Afterword

Dear Reader, thank you for taking this journey of discovering who the fugitives are in your life. I pray that you were encouraged to strip them of their power by choosing Jesus. I hope that in routing out these fugitives, you have reunited with God in every area of your heart. Always remember God's love for you. He spared no expense in redeeming you and yours from the enemy's clutch. He loves you with an everlasting love that is incomparable. There is a cloud of witnesses cheering you on as you walk this path. You will never be alone, and God himself will see you through every valley and peak of your life. God's love for you will heal, restore, break the bondage of cycles, unlock your identity and purpose, among other things. Paul states in Romans 8: 38-39, "For I am persuaded that neither death, nor life, nor angels nor principalities...nor any other created thing shall be able to separate us from the love of God which is in Christ Jesus." He has provided His son's blood so that you and I can meet him face to face without the hindrance of sin, iniquity, and transgression. I pray you feel that love and allow it to draw you to a deeper place in Him. The closer you are to God, the quicker the fugitives will dismantle. Their access to you will shrink and diminish as you grow in God. Let us take that step toward him; He is waiting with open arms. May we run into His arms and stay there forevermore, in Jesus' Name Amen.

More Resources

Here is a list of books that may help you in your walk with Jesus if you so desire. Some of them were already mentioned in this book.

Emotionally Healthy Spirituality. It's impossible to be spiritually mature while remaining emotionally immature. Peter Scazzero

Godly Relationships: A key to sexual fulfilment. Fransi Van Wyk

Repentance: Cleansing your generational bloodline, restoring the first state. Natasha Grbich

Overcoming Verdicts from the Courts of Hell. Dr. Ron. Horner

Unlocking Destinies from the Courts of Heaven: Dissolving curses that delay and deny our destinies. Robert Henderson

Wholeness: Winning life from the inside out. Touré Roberts

Index

Chapter 1: 2020

Scazzero, Peter. *Emotionally Healthy Spirituality: Unleash a Revolution in Your Life In Christ.* Zondervan, 2006, p. 12.

rockyverma4. "Its Better to Sit in a Bar Thinking about God than to Sit in a Church Thinking About?" *Reddit*, 2017, https://www.reddit.com/r/Showerthoughts/comments/5b2ehw/its_better_to_sit_in_a_bar_thinking_about_god/. Accessed March 11, 2021.

Unknown Author, "Draw a line in the sand"- anonymous

Chapter 2: Natural and Spiritual Functions of the heart

Nelson, Kevin. Abundant Life Church of Erie (ALCOE), 'God has to take time to clean the junk out', 'Salvation is progressive'.

Lewis. Tanya. Human Heart: Anatomy, Functions & Facts. https://www.livescience.com/34655-human-heart.html Assessed February 2021.

Chapter 3: Who Are the Fugitives?

Grbich, Natasha. *Repentance: Cleansing Your Generational Bloodline.* House of Ariel Gate, 2013, p.103.

Unknown Author, "Tell the truth and shame the devil"- anonymous

Burke, Edmund, "All that is necessary for the truimph of evil is that good men do nothing." https://www.padfield.com/1997/goodmen.html Accessed June, 16, 2021

Knight, Jeff, and Melinda. The Rock Church.

https://www.instagram.com/trclife/ Accessed January, 20, 2021

Perry-Hill, Jackie, "How can I serve a God that hasn't been able to change you"

https://www.instagram.com/jackiehillperry/ Accessed November 2020

"The Truth Doesn't Cost Anything but a Lie Will Cost You Everything." *Quoteistan*, 2016, https://www.quoteistan.com/2016/12/the-truth-doesnt-cost-anything-but-lie.html

Unknown Author, "It does not matter whether you are saved or not, everybody hates a liar"- anonymous

Fransi, Van Wyk. *Godly Relationships: A Key to Sexual Fulfilment.* House of Ariel Gate, 2018. Location 607 of 3528

Taken at Birth: Mausoleum Break-In (Season 1, Episode 2). TLC, 2019.

Henderson, Robert. *Unlocking Destinies From The Courts Of Heaven: Dissolving Curses That Delay and Deny Our Futures, Volume Two.* Robert Henderson Ministries, 2016, p.13.

"State Law Database: Laws In Your State." *RAINN*, 2021, https://apps.rainn.org/policy/.

"It Was Pride That Changed Angels into Devils; It Is Humility That Makes Men as Angels.' - Saint Augustine." *BrainyQuote*, https://www.brainyquote.com/quotes/saint_augustine_148546. Accessed 11 Mar. 2021.

"The things you take for granted, someone else is praying for"-Squeesome.com

https://medium.com/@treadmilltreats/the-things-you-take-for-granted-someone-else-is- praying-for-8500b22dc4ca Accessed April, 18, 2021

Merriam-Webster. 2021, https://www.merriam-webster.com/.

"'Ingratitude to Man Is Ingratitude to God.' — Samuel Ibn Naghrillah." *Quotefancy*, https://quotefancy.com/quote/1654688/Samuel-ibn-Naghrillah-Ingratitude-to-man-is-ingratitude-to-God %09. Accessed 11 Mar. 2021.

"'Saying Thank You Is More than Good Manners. It Is Good Spirituality.'— Alfred Agache." *Quotefancy*, https://quotefancy.com/quote/1573118/Alfred-Agache-Saying-thank-you-is-more-than-good-manners-It-is-good-spirituality. Accessed 11 Mar. 2021.

"'If You Don't like Something, Change It. If You Can't Change It, Change Your Attitude.' — Maya Angelou." *BrainyQuote*, https://www.brainyquote.com/quotes/maya_angelou_101310. Accessed 11 Mar. 2021.

Joyce Meyer. Do it Afraid. Embracing courage in the face of fear. Devotional. "You can't be delivered from something you refuse to admit" https://bible.com/r/5ca. Accessed October 31, 2020

"'Be Teachable. You're Not Always Right.'" *Pinterest*, https://www.pinterest.ca/pin/368380444522955205/. Accessed 12 Mar. 2021.

Monroe, Myles. *Applying the Kingdom: Rediscovering the Priority of God for Mankind*. Destiny Image Publishers, 2007.

Editors. History.com. Social Security Act. https://www.his-tory.com/topics/great-depression/social-security-act original 01/26/18. Updated 01/31/20. Accessed February 2021

Long. Nicole. What do our taxes pay for. https://www.sapling.com/7987574/services-do-taxes-pay. Accessed February 2021.

Dave Ramsey. Financial Peace University, "sell every-thing and make the kids think they'renext".https://www.ramseysolutions.com/ramseyplus/organization?int_cmp-gn=B2B Church Link RS Guides&int dept=rplus bu&int lctn=Homepage-Dave%27s Free Guides&int fmt=but-ton&int dscpn=Tracking all traffic that comes through the main %22for churches%22 link on the RS guides page.&campaign_id=7011Y000001bpIv&lead_source=Direct. Accessed June 7, 2021

Chapter 6: What Now?

Merriam-Webster. 2021, https://www.merriam-webster.com/.

Horner, Ron M. *Overcoming Verdicts from the Courts of Hell: Releasing False Judgments*. LifeSpring Publishing, 2016, p. 94.

HUB Global Reformers Summit. Henderson, Robert. Watkins, Beverly. Tyre, Jacquie. Unlocking the Courts of Heaven. https://globalreformers.com/summit-meetings. Attended May 4-6, 2017

West, Matthew, "Something to say"

CPSIA information can be obtained
at www.ICGtesting.com
Printed in the USA
BVHW082053240921
617501BV00002B/257

9 781662 824074